FAMILY SUCCESS

Building a Legacy Takes More than Money

SCOTT D. SERFASS

To my family and friends.
I owe my success to you.
Thank you for your loyalty and support.

PREFACE

Success isn't a result of spontaneous combustion.
You must set yourself on fire.
—Arnold H. Glasow

Have you ever wondered how to prepare your children for success? How to build a strong family bond? How to create a legacy that helps future generations seek happiness? As a financial planner, I often hear questions such as these from parents and grandparents as we discuss their financial future and legacy. Over the course of the last decade, I have seen many families grow stronger through the ebbs and flows of the economy and financial markets, while others have seen their wealth diminish. What was the difference?

You, like many others, might guess poor investment strategies, an ill-advised estate plan, or lack of a plan in general. While this might be true for some, it is typically a very small percentage. More often, there is another reason why three out of four families see their wealth destroyed by the time it transfers to the third generation: human behavior.

Naturally, most parents think about their legacy later in life. In the early years, they worry about buying their first home, getting kids through school, and eventually retiring. Children leave the nest, perhaps having children of their own. Some end up successful, while others are still "finding their way." Parents then develop an estate plan for money to flow from one generation to the next. The typical flaw in the plan, though, is the preparation of future generations to handle money and success.

A growing body of research in behavioral finance continues to uncover how and why we make everyday money decisions. These studies often focus on how our brains are wired and how our backgrounds shape financial decisions. To put it simply, creating and maintaining wealth is just as much about our personal characteristics as it is about our financial education. My unique position in wealth management has allowed me to observe some of the common traits in families having multigenerational success: drive, emotional balance, creativity, and influence.

I, like many of you parents and grandparents, want nothing more than to help my future generations get whatever they want in life. I want a plan to build the characteristics and skills that lead to success. I want future generations to feel a sense of pride about their family, and I want my success to be a starting point for wealth that lasts many lifetimes. The chapters following will reveal strategies to do just that.

Building family success takes vision. The thought process behind leaving a legacy is different and even a little uncomfortable to some. But how many families can actually answer my initial three questions? I wrote this book for people like you and me: those that want to shift the odds of success in their favor as early as possible.

The beauty of humanity is that it is perfectly imperfect. There is no one-size-fits-all approach. However, I hope this book lays the groundwork for you to plan your family's future success. Thanks for reading!

CONTENTS

INTRODUCTION

Family success and wealth are not self-perpetuating. Today's modern family faces struggles that previous generations never thought possible. With the divorce rate in America steadily climbing, the number of adults experiencing multiple marriages—and the subsequent blending of families—has all but become commonplace. An increase in biracial, same-sex, and inter-faith marriages also creates confusion and uncertainty as families search to find their own identity. We all have obstacles to overcome while striving to improve future generations. Let's face it; our families are never going to be perfect. I'm reminded of this by the pillow that sits on my grandmother's rocking chair displaying the phrase "My family tree is full of nuts."

Evenings spent sitting together around the dinner table discussing the day have fallen by the wayside as well. In the past 20 years, the frequency of family dinners have declined, with only a third of American families sitting down together. When those families do break bread, the average time spent at the table is 30 minutes or less—one-third the length of a typical family dinner in the 1950s. Dinner was once a sacred time. Phones were unplugged, televisions were turned off, and everyone recounted the day's events. Today, you are more likely to see a family sitting in a restaurant completely oblivious to anything around them except the phones in their hands.

As family communication continues to decline, our children are replacing it with messages from other, often unidentified sources. With the onslaught of new technologies, teens today spend about seven and a half hours each day consuming messages from various television shows, social media sites, and the Internet. Innovative target marketing tactics help companies get into the minds of these young people. Airbrushed celebrities showing off their perfect bodies and sex appeal, the "cool" factor of drinking a Starbucks coffee or alcohol, and the constant focus on materialism as the primary source of happiness in one's life are adding new obstacles to the family dynamic.

This demise of traditional family values is beginning to have a profound effect on a new, unsuspecting class of children—the affluent. These families (generally at least \$100,000 in liquid assets or \$75,000 in annual income) are beginning to face the double-edged sword of their elevated status in life. Researchers are finding that growing up in an affluent home increases psychosocial risks, including substance abuse, depression, and anxiety. These symptoms often develop from the constant pressure to achieve as well as isolation (both literal and emotional) from the children's often busy parents.

Subsequently, drug use and suicide are becoming more prevalent among younger generations. According to the National Institute on Drug Abuse (NIDA), illegal drug usage among teenagers has risen in the past 20 years and remains high, most notably due to the popularization and recent legalization of marijuana in some states. Teen suicide continues to climb and is now the second leading cause of death among young people ages 15 to 24.

James, a high school senior living in a Chicago suburb, sees these issues firsthand among his fellow classmates. While his family would generally be considered middle class, he cites a vast majority of his friends come from wealthier backgrounds where money is no object, parental involvement is minimal, and consequences for troubling behavior are laughable. James is an intelligent young man and a great athlete, but his involvement with this troubling group sent him down a path of destruction.

His friends are typically given money without question, often lying about going to the movies and instead buying alcohol or drugs for the next party. James witnesses many of his peers "medicating" daily, sometimes just to pass the time while doing homework or to deal with anxiety. "The people doing this every day are the ones that have the money to support the habit and tend to use it as a means of stress relief," he adds.

While alcohol and marijuana are most common, wealthier students are also resorting to prescription drugs such as Xanax and Adderall. These medications are often used during finals when academic stress is at an all-time high, but many also mix them with alcohol and marijuana to create a greater "relaxing" effect during parties. James recalls one student taking so many Xanax throughout the school day that he could not recall his own name. While drugs and alcohol have long been a part of the experimentation phase of teenagers, this new reliance and search for a stronger high or buzz is a troubling trend. The absence of parental guidance is often the cited cause of this effect.

Shirtsleeves to Shirtsleeves in Three Generations

Reports suggest 70% of these affluent, successful families find their wealth diminished by the time it reaches the third generation—less than 3% of these families citing imprudent financial strategies as the cause. Given the troubling trends we just discussed, it is no surprise family success is difficult to maintain. The lack of focus on the behavioral side of success and wealth management stacks the odds against your hard work and daily sacrifice providing for many generations to come. Hence, the old adage "shirtsleeves to shirtsleeves in three generations" has been around for centuries.

This phenomenon is not just found in the United States but across the globe. The Spanish say, "Quien no lo tiene, lo hace; y quien lo tiene, lo deshace" ("who doesn't have it, does it, and who has it, misuses it"). Italians use "Dalle stele alle stalle" ("from stars to stalls"). Regardless of the translation, the story remains the same. The first generation finds success by literally or figuratively rolling up their shirt sleeves. They work hard, often sacrificing lifestyle for the betterment of their financial future. Through the development of a successful business or just old-fashioned savings, wealth is accumulated.

The second generation is then able to reap the rewards of this newfound status. They attend better schools, have access to more influential people, and find success as the hardworking values and ideals of the first generation have been engrained in them for many years. For some families, the second generation will deplete the wealth of the first in an effort to continue to build status. The accumulation of material goods often becomes more important than the accumulation of wealth.

If there happens to be money left over for the third generation, this is where it frequently disappears. The third generation grows up with the "silver spoon" feeding them from day one. They live a life of luxury, having never witnessed the sacrifice of the first generation. They drive to private school in a BMW and go to the family beach house during the summer. Would they dare take a job out of college for a measly $30,000 per year? How could they afford the "finer things" on such a salary? Their high standard of living is not sustainable on their own, and consequently, the remaining wealth is often used to try to maintain it. For these families, the focus is all wrong.

How do we cultivate future generations with so many outside forces working against us? These stories and statistics highlight the most important factor of family success and wealth—the people within it. Whether you are trying to continue your family's current success or simply helping the next generation be better than the last, the proactive building of human and intellectual capital is a must. You can give your children the best education money can buy and the best investment strategies to grow wealth, but if you do not focus on developing the characteristics of successful people, you set your family up to become just another statistic.

My Success Is Not Your Success

Success carries many definitions depending on who you ask. People often judge achievement externally by looking at money, power, or status. The car you drive or the career title you hold can be all you need to seem successful on the surface. Yet if you ask someone who is truly accomplished to define this phenomenon, the acquisition of material items is rarely high on the list. Success is often more about the journey than the outcome. You are more likely to hear words such as passion, fulfillment, and hard work from these individuals. Your idea of success is going to be different from mine. That's the beauty of it. We all have our personal version of happiness. Thus, as we discuss family success, the goal is not to determine the end result for our children or grandchildren but to give them the tools needed to paint their own picture. Defining success for others then needs to be put into a different perspective.

*Success is passionately pursuing
meaningful work at a high level.*

Think about it: The people that love what they do are not watching the clock, counting down the minutes before they can go home, or daydreaming about retirement. Talk to someone you define as successful and you'll likely see their enthusiasm and passion pour from them as they talk about their work. Without that excitement, working at a high level is very difficult due to the time and energy it takes to achieve success.

As a parent, it is your job to prepare your children to find their purpose and help them understand what it will take to produce at this high level. But how do you begin to assist a child with achieving their dream? First and foremost, you must be a guide to help determine what goals, dreams, and aspirations they have in life. Do they have an interest in science? The arts? The outdoors? Understanding what drives your child can help turn a passion into a meaningful career path.

Wharton professor Richard Shell outlines the three components of truly meaningful work in his book, *Springboard*:

- **Reward-Driven:** work others will reward you for (i.e., financial compensation and/or affirmation or praise)
- **Talent-Driven:** work that utilizes your talents and strengths (i.e., a child that is a great public speaker may think about a career in politics)
- **Emotionally-Driven:** work you are passionate about, whether you are paid for it or not (i.e., an activity your child would perform with excitement and not worry about gaining anything—financially or otherwise)

When these three elements come together, true success and career happiness are often the byproduct. Successful families understand the underlying difficulty of this process. The biggest obstacle? The average epidemic.

Family Beware

The average epidemic is making it challenging to stand out from the crowd. When successful people break the mold and make a name for themselves, the bar is raised, thus shifting the bell curve for others. Achievers are often met by naysayers pressuring them to "fit in" with the crowd. This animosity and jealousy can derail potential success, especially for children.

Madi is a straight-A student and, in 2014, received the honor of "Terrific Kid of the Year" in her fifth-grade class in South Carolina. This award is one of many she typically receives for her excellence in academics. Classmates and friends, however, have become jealous of her success, causing Madi to feel embarrassed and self-conscious of her achievements. When presented with the award at the school assembly, she noticed her best friends were not clapping for her. She overheard one girl say, "Madi wins *everything*," to which another replied, "I know. It's so annoying."

Madi works diligently to get good grades. She is a seemingly rare breed who reads for fun and enjoys learning about new subjects in her spare time. Madi should be celebrating her awards, not hiding from them. Yet her consistent over-achievement is a stress to her ability to fit in. She has been known to tell her teachers to give her awards to other children as she already has enough. Her parents worry this pressure will keep her from continuing to stand out academically.

The epidemic's goal is to create a world in which everyone is special. By this very definition, however, if everyone is special, then no one is special. We suppress great performance with less recognition and send a message to the stragglers that it is fine to be below average. Just one year prior, Madi was awarded the "Citizenship Award," the highest honor earned in fourth grade. She was recognized and given the award in private so no other students would know and feel left out.

Sports are also a big target of the average epidemic. Not keeping score, trophies for participation, and even penalties for spectators cheering are sheltering children from dealing with adversity and losing. Children need to learn how to overcome obstacles and experience failure, and this can be done productively in sports with support from parents, coaches, and teachers. Instead of teaching how to better support children in sports, society finds it easier to just eliminate the stress or problem. What is this saying to the children striving for success?

Family Success

Building a successful family means challenging ordinary expectations. An average family learns to live within its means, understanding that resources are fixed and hard to come by. While this strategy can lead to a healthy balance sheet and retirement for the first generation, it will usually not create a lasting legacy. A successful family learns to produce the wealth needed to accomplish their goals and lifestyle. They see success as an endless resource and roadblocks as a barrier to entry, not a reason to give up.

These families also understand that school is important but not the only means of becoming successful. What good is it to be able to name all of the generals of the Civil War if a child doesn't know how to properly write a resume or speak effectively in front of an audience? In fact, today more companies are focusing on personality tests, work ethic, and signs of resilience rather than a resume littered with personal accomplishments. Richard Anderson, CEO of Delta Airlines, notes:

> You have to probe a little deeper into the human intangibles, because we've all seen many instances where people had perfect resumes but weren't effective in an organization. So it's not just education and experience. It's education, experience, and the human factor—the situational awareness that a person has and

that person's ability to fit into an organization and then be successful in the organization. It's a whole series of intangibles that are almost gut instincts about people.

Instead of focusing solely on grades and performance, parents can better serve their children by developing the intangible qualities of success. High achievers have characteristics that don't come from a textbook. They are hardworking and passionately driven. They are able to deal with stressful situations and challenging people. They think outside the box and are able to persuade people to take action or follow them. Good grades and extracurricular achievements may get you in the game, but it doesn't necessarily make you a successful player today. It is time we shift focus.

Cultivating Internal Drive

Parents cannot force a child to be driven. It is a characteristic that needs to be led by example and cultivated in a child's life. Ted Ligety, U.S. alpine ski racer, is a two-time Olympic gold medalist and in 2013 became the first man in 45 years to win gold in three alpine events at a single world championship.

Surprisingly, he was not always a skiing prodigy. When Ted began to seriously compete in downhill racing, he remembers not only losing to the younger boys but the girls as well. At age 11, he was losing races by as much as seven seconds, which in downhill skiing is a lifetime.

Ligety often cites his parents as the driving force behind his success: "They taught me the importance of hard work and independence.... They made ski racing my own thing. They never pushed me. They just encouraged me. [They] helped me develop into a well-rounded person as well." Ted also notes if his parents tried to push him into skiing, he would have likely rebelled and not have had the same passion for the sport.

Instilling natural drive in your children involves an approach beyond the old "carrot and stick" methods. It takes a delicate balance of success and failure. It takes a growth-oriented mindset. It takes a parent letting go of control and helping their children find independence.

Building Emotional Balance

The average epidemic represents a much larger issue. Sheltering children from feeling sadness, anger, frustration, or jealousy is not helping them cope with adversity later in life. These emotions are unavoidable, and our reactions to them are important for dealing with the hardships that come with success.

Social media is a great example of how success subjects you to the emotional terrorism of others. Celebrities and athletes are often targets of criticism, name calling, or even worse, threats. During the 2013 NFL season, Brandon Jacobs, running back for the NY Giants, posted a picture of a tweet sent by a disgruntled fantasy football player. This message threatened the lives of Brandon and his family if he did not rush for 50 yards against the Vikings. It takes an emotionally balanced person to deal with such negativity, and whether you are a NFL running back like Brandon or a great student like Madi, success will eventually test your emotions.

Since the early 1990s, parents and teachers have continued to lead a movement to remove certain games and activities that can cause emotional stress from school curricula. Neil F. Williams, professor at Eastern Connecticut State University, proclaimed that games such as dodgeball, duck-duck-goose, tag, and kickball should be added to his ever-growing list of ego-cutting games in his controversial article, "The Physical Education Hall of Shame." The purpose of eliminating such games is to avoid singling out children and hurting feelings.

Opponents, however, see this change as a contributing factor to the "wussification of America." How are we to teach our children to handle disappointment, rise through adversity, or value hard work if we take away a great illustration all children can comprehend—competitive play? If we want our children to be emotionally balanced, the answer does not lie in sheltering them from life. We need to teach them *how* to use all their emotions—the good, the bad, and the ugly.

Inspiring Creativity

Many people today think creativity is something you are born with—you either have it or you don't. The ability to innovate or solve complex problems are tasks for only a few select individuals with the creative gene. However, research is proving the opposite to be true. Creativity can be nurtured from a young age as it has been defined as a process rather than a fixed trait. Much like a musician or an athlete improving their craft through deliberate practice, understanding the process of creativity can help your family become better innovators and problem solvers. Evidence, however, points to children's creativity being stifled today.

After the implementation of the *No Child Left Behind Act*, schools started lessening the time for "free play" to focus students' attention on math and reading to bolster standardized test scores. Timothy Osberg, professor of psychology at Niagara University, counters, "Play is a major mechanism in how we learn social skills and how we develop creativity."

Schools are not the only culprits. Parents over-scheduling children with structured, extra-curricular activities are further adding to the issue. Boredom, while often considered negative, can actually be a great way for children to get creative. Without this freedom of time, we are robbing our children of creative practice and potentially our futures from new technological, scientific, and sociological developments.

Take Twitter for example. One of the most well-known social media sites today was actually conceptualized on a playground. The then podcasting company was on the brink of disaster, faced with fierce competition from Apple. During a lunch break, Jack Dorsey, the co-founder and co-creator of Twitter, thought of the idea of creating a site that would act as "a dispatch service that connects us on our phones using text" while sitting on a slide! Thanks to his unorthodox pit stop that day, Twitter—and a new way of sharing information— was born.

As Jack Dorsey proves, creativity is not just about art, music, or design. Understanding the process improves everyday problem-solving skills and inspires life-long learning. Thus, your role as "creative facilitator" is an important one.

Being a Positive Influence

Words have power: the power to build up, the power to tear down, and the power to influence. During a study performed by a research team at the University of Pittsburgh School of Medicine, participants were divided into two groups and given the same hypothetical scenario: A loved one had just been in a horrific accident. It was up to the family to decide to continue treatment or sign a do-not-resuscitate order (DNR).

Group A was approached by an actor posing as a doctor and asked whether they wanted CPR to be performed if their loved one's heart stopped or if they would sign a DNR. Close to 60% chose to have CPR administered.

Group B was approached by the same "doctor"; however, this time, he changed his wording. Instead of asking the family members if they would sign a DNR, he asked if they would like to allow the patient a "natural death" rather than utilize CPR. This time, only 49% chose the CPR option.

Simple words in this example can save a life or end one. A doctor's ability to persuade patients to lead a healthier life, take prescription drugs, or make life-altering decisions lies in the ability to establish credibility, build a trusting relationship, and communicate in an effective manner. New research suggests that 85% of an individual's success in business is attributed to his or her ability to persuade and influence. Not everyone wants to be a leader or is cut out for the job, but influencing others is part of everyday life and a skill needed by younger generations to thrive.

As a parent, I imagine you want your children to *have* positive influences in their lives as well as *be* a positive influence to others. The old saying, "Do as I say, not as I do," does not work with children. They are watching your every move. We as parents and individuals are far from perfect, but they should witness you striving for continuous improvement and taking ownership of your mistakes. Understanding the essence of true influence is the key to setting a good example and helping your children develop this important skill.

Creating an Environment for Success

How does a family go from a disconnected group of people with separate ideas and expectations about life to a close, united team? John Davison Rockefeller, Sr., founded the Rockefeller family fortune in the late 1800s. Because of his business expertise, he became the nation's wealthiest man by the time of his death in 1937. His only son, John D. Rockefeller, Jr., was not interested in business like his father however. Realizing this, John Sr. helped his son find his calling by concentrating and developing his passions— philanthropic efforts and family. John Jr. wanted to make sure his father's legacy and hard-earned money stretched beyond the next generation; he wanted his children's, children's, children to be able to— literally—*share the Rockefeller wealth.*

Rockefeller Jr. created a family office to assist in managing the family fortune with the primary goal being to foster and promote growth among individual members. One of the keys to achieving this objective was creating a successful family meeting. The virtues of this meeting continue today as Rockefeller members meet to discuss individual, generational, and family-wide concerns. Each member has a role, knows their purpose, and understands the importance of a united front. It has not always been easy, but this has ensured the endurance of the family fortune as well as cleared the lines of communication among individual family members. The family meeting is the final difference between a family like the Rockefellers and one that eventually falls victim to the *shirtsleeves to shirtsleeves* prophecy.

Successful families celebrate their uniqueness but work hard to maintain close relationships *despite* their differences. The intent is not to force family members to conform to a single mold but to strive for advancement together. Nurturing internal drive, fostering emotional balance, cultivating creativity, developing influence, and implementing strategic family meetings can help overcome the odds of generational failure and send your family's success soaring.

How do we use these building blocks to create a sturdy foundation for generational success? In the following chapters, you will find actionable ways to improve your family's future by drawing upon my experience in wealth management along with the experience of other experts in the fields of psychology, business, motivation, and neuroscience. Let's get started.

CHAPTER ONE

DRIVE

Successful people work hard long before they see fame and fortune. We often observe the finish line of an individual's success but do not always see the blood, sweat, and tears. Olympic Alpine skier Ted Ligety did not wait for good luck to shine down on him. He didn't throw a penny into a wishing well and hope that someday he would become an Olympic gold medalist. He worked hard, he was determined to meet his goal, and he did not let negativity affect his resolve to be the best.

When Ligety was 11 years old, however, his parents thought his dreams of being an Olympic skier were over. He was not chosen to ski with the Olympic prodigies in his hometown of Park City, UT, and was told by several coaches that the Olympics were not in his future. "They would say, 'No, Ted, set a realistic goal,'" his mother, Cyndi Sharp, recounts. But Ted would not give up. His goal was to be an Olympian. He continued to push himself to improve every day.

While families tend to share many traits, individuals can have very different talents, passions, and thoughts on success. Some parents think of their lives as a predetermined script and thus think the same for future generations. However, people like Ligety do not see life this way. They take control and fuel their passion to achieve the result they desire. Helping your children develop the drive to pursue their passions is a key ingredient to success as a family. In his book, *Drive*, Daniel Pink explains this phenomenon of internal motivation using three simple ingredients: autonomy, mastery, and purpose. Ted Ligety owned all three.

Autonomy

When asked what led to Ligety's drive and determination, his mother, Cyndi, replied simply, "He was raised to be very independent." Autonomy is the sense of personal choice and control. One of the biggest threats to a child's ability to attain autonomy is an overprotective parent— the helicopter parent. This anxious parent hovers closely over their child's head (literally and metaphorically), trying to control every situation possible. They work tirelessly to ensure their child never endures an ounce of pain or disappointment, often continuing this pattern well into adulthood.

Eleanor Green, a Boston restaurateur, has witnessed this firsthand as she recalls an interview with a college student. "[The parent said], 'I'm here with my son, Mark, to apply for a bus boy position.' Mark is standing there not saying a word. We're thinking if Mark can't talk to us, how can he interact with our staff and customers?"

College administrator Terry Jordan also cites an increasing number of helicopter parents getting involved with their college-aged children at the University of North Carolina–Charlotte. He recently reviewed an email from a parent requesting an exception for her son who just received his second D in freshman English. The excuse? "He is now realizing that he has to *work* in college to pass."

While protecting a child from hardships may seem like it is in their best interest, this behavior could actually be detrimental. A growing body of evidence continues to highlight the negative side effects of the helicopter parent with little argument to the contrary. Children with over-protective parents tend to exhibit traits such as narcissism, anxiety, stress, and poor coping and decision-making skills in adulthood.

Mastery

Mastery is the comprehensive knowledge and skill of a subject and it is essential to success in today's world. The idea of someone being a "natural" is largely misunderstood. When parents see their child struggle at a new activity, they may think there is a lack of natural talent and suggest moving on. While certain attributes may make us better suited for certain tasks, no one starts at the top. Being tall may make you better suited to play basketball, but you are not born with basketball skills. It takes practice.

Ted Ligety was not at the top of his ski class growing up. Ligety saw his ability as improvable and therefore did not let the initial failure get in the way of his ultimate goal. To foster this quest for mastery, parents must instill what Carol S. Dweck, a leading researcher of motivation, calls the growth mindset. Those with a growth mindset view their personal qualities as flexible; they are adaptable to change through hard work, experience, and application. These people see challenges as a chance to learn, not as a reflection of their personal worth.

The opposing force to the growth mindset is the thought that "we are who we are, and that's the way it is"—a fixed mindset. Those suffering from this frame of mind, feel the need to prove themselves worthy and superior in every area of life. When faced with difficulty, they typically respond to the challenges as though they are personal attacks. They feel their personality and mental qualities are fixed and intractable; thus, they need to defend them rather than seek feedback to improve.

Mastery is a driving force to self-confidence. When you feel prepared, you give yourself permission to achieve at a high level. An experienced doctor will be more at ease when emergencies arise, just as memorizing and practicing your speech before a big presentation will help calm your nerves when it comes time to stand up in front of the crowd. Mastery makes winning an expectation. Parents can focus on creating an environment that fosters a growth mindset to allow their child to feel more in control of their development and build the self-confidence that comes from hard work and achievement.

Purpose

Purpose gives a deeper meaning and connection to our work but is often not easily understood. Some people seem to have always known exactly what they want to do in life, while others struggle to find significance. Helping your child find purpose could be the greatest thing you do as a parent. Ligety began skiing at the age of two. Tiger Woods was introduced to golf even earlier. These stories are often highlighted by the media, largely because they are anomalies. It is a common misconception that one needs to start at a very early age to find success. In fact, a vast majority of professional athletes did not start this early.

For purpose to be powerful, though, it needs to include a cause bigger than ourselves. It could be as simple as leaving a meaningful legacy for our family or impacting others through our work. Regardless, this focus on the greater good will keep the fire burning bright. Aside from skiing, Ligety is involved in designing ski apparel with Shred Optics and volunteering with Youth Enrichment Services to help urban children learn to ski and snowboard. He uses his celebrity-like status to enrich the lives of others.

Your child's purpose will become apparent when their passion meets their personal strengths. Encouraging your child to experience new things and independently seek activities they truly enjoy can be a great start. You will likely see a purpose develop as enthusiasm and excitement become more apparent.

The Carrot and the Stick Won't Do the Trick

The "carrot and the stick" is a regularly cited method for motivating. It refers to a cart driver dangling a carrot in front of a mule and holding a stick behind it. The mule moves toward the carrot, thus pulling the cart in hopes of a tasty reward, the stinging "thwap" of the stick is to be used if the tasty reward is no longer compelling enough for the mule to move forward. This is a productive means for motivating short-term, remedial tasks, but it will never turn the mule into a thoroughbred.

The carrot, from a parenting perspective, generally takes the form of a good old-fashioned bribe. "Pick up all your toys and you'll get a piece of candy" may work as a means to get your children to clean their room, but this tactic does little to change behavior or performance long term.

Likewise, the "stick" can also be an effective means to compel your child to act. I, like many of us who grew up prior to the '90s, faced a spanking on numerous occasions. It only took one or two before the mere threat would send me straight into compliance. While spanking is not a preferred parenting discipline today, the threat of punishment can be a great motivator for children. But when the catalyst no longer exists, will they remain motivated to continue the preferred behavior?

If a parent truly desires to raise a motivated child, *they* are the ones that need to make changes. Parents want to step in at the first sign of trouble and control every situation. The child wants to assert his or her independence. It was renowned family therapist Salvador Minuchin who said, "Parents cannot protect and guide without controlling and restricting. Children cannot become individuals without resisting and attacking.

The process of child rearing is, therefore, inherently conflictual."

Building Drive

Allow the Struggle...

Parents need to let their children struggle. For some, especially the affluent, it is often easier to step in and quickly solve everyday issues. But just like the "carrot and the stick" catalyst, a parent will not be able to do this forever. Successful families help children learn that all things in life will not come easy, but with perseverance, they can accomplish their goals.

Allowing a child to make mistakes and endure the natural consequences of their actions will better build decision-making skills. James, the suburban high school senior introduced previously, was arrested for underage drinking and possession of marijuana twice. The first time, through a wealthier friend's connection, a big-shot lawyer was hired to help his case. James was given a laughable slap on the wrist because, as the judge said, "You're lucky you know this guy [the lawyer]."

Unfortunately, James did not learn his lesson and was later arrested again. His parents made him take full responsibility for his actions this time around. James had to sell his car and work to pay for all legal fees and fines he accrued. They finally realized rescuing their precious child from every bad situation was not teaching him proper values. Many of the affluent parents in their network praised them for disciplining James despite citing that they did not have the strength to do the same to their children.

... But Not Too Much

While it is important to struggle to build resilience, children also need to succeed and feel supported. While James's parents let him feel the harsh realities of his actions, they continued to support him by being with him in court and providing assurance that if he learns from this, success is still a possibility. Positive reinforcement from parents is an important balance to allowing the struggle. Without it, learned helplessness can occur.

Brian Tracy, highly regarded motivational speaker and author, recounts his experience with learned helplessness during his travels to India:

> When elephant trainers in India catch a baby elephant, they tie one of its legs to a post with a rope. The baby elephant struggles and struggles but it can't get free. For days the baby elephant pulls and strains at the rope. Gradually it learns that struggle is useless and it gives up.
>
> When the elephant grows up, the trainer keeps it tied to the same rope in the same way. And even though it can now break the rope and get away, it stands passively and waits for

the trainer to come and get it. It has developed what is called learned helplessness. It has learned that the struggle is useless. As a result of repeated failed experiences earlier in life, the elephant has learned a self-imposed limitation.

With too many struggles, children can become helpless just like the trained elephant. Richard Lavoie, author of *The Motivation Breakthrough*, also notes that continuous failure sets the expectation that the child will continue to fail at similar tasks in the future. Lavoie recalls this experience when teaching a math class several years ago. When he announced they were going to try something new today, his student, Craig, immediately raised his hand stating that he could not complete the task and would need help. Craig's constant failure in math led him to raise the white flag in defeat before the assignment was even explained.

Ensure that your child's goals are challenging but achievable. If a child believes that their best attempts at something will not allow them to achieve, they will inevitably give up. Do not progress a child too far, too fast. Skipping grades or competing with older children in sports is great but only if it is put into perspective and the opportunity to succeed still exists.

Positive Behavior Modification

A child's inner dialogue is often a reflection of his or her environment. A parent's positive or negative speak can have great influence over time. Imagine being a 13 year-old playing on the middle school basketball team. You are about to shoot two free throws with the game on the line. Your coach brings everyone into the huddle to discuss the strategy and then looks to you and says, "Don't miss this shot!"

Are the thoughts running through your head positive or negative? Instead of focusing on making the free throws, your mind is now focusing on not missing. The pressure to not miss that shot—or any "shot" you take in life—can be overwhelming. Your inner dialogue is most often the greatest determinant of your actions and the eventual outcome. Professional athletes are often seen as overconfident or arrogant, but that confidence is what allows them to compete at a high level. They believe they are the best and will win. Parents can help infuse this positive attitude by rephrasing how they speak to their child. "When you make this shot..." encourages the right frame of mind to approach the free throw.

Conversely, when your child is acting rebellious, expressing the behavior you would like to see exhibited will have a more lasting effect with less room for creative interpretation. During the summer months, parents are often heard around the pool yelling, "Stop running!" The child then typically changes from a running motion to a fast-paced, Jazzercise-like walking motion. "*Walk* around the pool" positively articulates the behavior that is expected and leaves little room for hopping, skipping, or other moves resembling a cheesy '80s exercise class.

Reinforcing the behavior you expect instead of strictly reprimanding the action you see, provides greater clarity to your child.

Be Mindful of Praise

Though continuous nagging can be damaging, the opposite—excessive praise—can be just as detrimental to motivation. Columbia University research suggests students given excess praise regarding their intelligence became more anxious about their results over time. This anxiety led them to forgo great learning opportunities at the risk of making mistakes or receiving less than stellar grades. Improper praise can lead children to perform for the approval of others and focus on the result rather than continuous development. Alfie Kohn, a leader in progressive education, feels praise increases a child's dependence on adults and their approval. Children need unconditional love, support, and encouragement, but they also need feedback.

Children should be encouraged to please themselves, not to please others. Saying "*You* worked hard to get good grades; *you* should be proud of yourself!" versus "I'm proud of your good grades" creates the desire to work hard to accomplish goals without needing the affirmation of others. Elizabeth Hartley-Brewer, an advisor on children's learning and development, surveyed a group of teens and found their least favorite praise was "I'm proud of you."

Comments specifically tailored to their accomplishment, such as "I'm proud of how hard you played in the soccer game today" or "You must be proud of making the honor roll," scored the highest.

Relinquish Some Control

Like Ted Ligety, leadership expert John Maxwell attributes his success to his father allowing him to be independent while growing up. "I never consciously limited you as long as I knew what you were doing was morally right," Maxwell recalls his father telling him. This autonomy served him well as he went on to sell over 18 million leadership books and has been seen on *The New York Times*, *The Wall Street Journal*, and *BusinessWeek's* best sellers lists. Children need choices to feel in control of their lives. If they are never given an opportunity to make decisions, how will they fare when they enter adulthood and no longer have guidance?

Even the simplest of choices can help a child feel independent. Allowing your youngster to choose today's outfit may seem like a small gesture but can help build autonomous thinking. If you do not want your child dressing up as Batman or a princess, give them two or three suitable options instead. Include your children in larger decisions as well, like planning the family vacation. Present options with a budget, and allow them to help plan the excursion. Getting your children involved in everyday decision making will make them feel more a part of the family and further develop decisiveness along the way.

Family Chores

Children have the right to share in the family's financial resources such as food, clothing, vacations, etc. But they should also have the responsibility to *contribute* to the family. Chores are a part of everyday life and should be an obligation of every family member. They bring a sense of accountability and accomplishment, which plays a vital role in a child's development.

Dr. Marty Rossman, associate professor of family education at the University of Minnesota, found children who started doing work around the house by the age of 3 or 4 were more successful in early adulthood. The study also found waiting to assign chores until your children are teenagers had an adverse effect, and the group was less successful later in life.

Chores teach children life skills: cooking, cleaning, doing laundry, etc. They also promote primary work attitudes such as dependability, responsibility, and attention to detail. These skills are transferrable to school and later to the job force. Family chores create fundamental work habits and are easy to implement at an early age.

Allowance

My experience in wealth management has made me an advocate of giving children an allowance as soon as they begin to question the concept of money. Not only does it teach basic money management, but it also teaches self-control and delayed gratification. Parents often misuse an allowance, however, by treating it as an external motivation tool—a carrot.

For instance, paying for good grades sounds like a great way to push your child to be a better student, but it can actually "cheapen" the task at hand. Money is often used to pay for services you do not want to do yourself. I pay someone to mow my lawn because I feel my time is better spent with family, completing other projects, or growing my business. Giving your children five dollars for every "A" on a report card gives them the impression that getting good grades is a chore, not something you do to advance your education and future.

If implemented correctly, allowances can be a great teaching tool and satisfy the need for control and autonomy. Allowances should start out small and be associated with a particular everyday expense. Perhaps your child gets a snack or toy when you go to the grocery store. Give them two dollars next visit and allow them to pick out the item of their choice while staying within the budget.

As your child grows up, the dollar amount and responsibility of the allowance should grow as well.

Allowances can cover expenses such as movies with friends, lunch at school, iTunes purchases, or clothing. Pre-paid cards can be a great starter for learning about credit cards and will save you a conversation about the $100 iTunes bill this month. When your child frivolously spends their allowance (and they will) only to find themselves out of money for the next great purchase, do not give a cash advance. It was your child's fault for not budgeting properly, not yours. With independence comes responsibility for your actions. An allowance is a cheap way to teach this.

Reality Check

Allowances are a great way for children to learn the value of a dollar. But parents should also be sure to teach the value of working for something—or someone— without expecting anything in return. Volunteer work or community service helps a child develop empathy, embrace working for the betterment of something other than themselves, and develop a perspective of the everyday struggles people encounter.

As the net worth of a family grows, children can easily have a misunderstanding of the "real world." Considering that over 80% of today's millionaires did not consider their family to be wealthy growing up, money is often taken for granted by younger generations being born into a successful family. You can tell your child they have a great life until you are blue in the face, but it will be difficult for them to understand until they witness the life of someone less fortunate.

Research concludes that children that perform community service on a *consistent* basis show an increase in physiological well-being and academic functioning. It puts into perspective the often trivial roadblocks or stresses we encounter on a daily basis. There is nothing more sobering than talking to someone with a disability or a teenager overcoming abuse. Community service teaches your child there is a world that does not revolve around them.

Luck Is a Four-Letter Word

As someone who enjoys the game of golf, I often hear the phrase "It's better to be lucky than good." But is it? I would much rather be good at something than lucky! But performing at a high level also takes a big commitment. As first-century Roman philosopher Seneca stated, "Luck is where the crossroads of opportunity and preparation meet." Ted Ligety believed he could win, and he was prepared when he got his chance. Help your child understand the future is in their control, but great performance does not come naturally—it takes commitment. Focus on developing autonomy, building mastery, and finding purpose. Do not let them be a part of the "it's better to be lucky than good" crowd, because it's not.

CHAPTER TWO

EMOTIONAL BALANCE

Everyone faces challenges they need to overcome. For children, challenges can come in the form of learning disabilities or family issues. Other times, they stem from social trials. How children react to these situations can greatly factor into mental health and future success. Parents naturally want to shelter children from the hardships of the world; however, this tendency is hindering their emotional development and ability to one day become productive adults.

Our society seems to focus on removing negative stimuli instead of teaching children how to overcome them or act appropriately. Why? Perhaps it is the path of least resistance or possibly an overreaction to rare incidents. Such is the case of the old schoolyard game of dodgeball.

Dodgeball was brought to America over 100 years ago and has long since been a staple of PE classes around the country. In the last 20 years, the game has been put under heavy scrutiny since professor Neil F. Williams added it to his controversial "Physical Education Hall of Shame." For a game to qualify for this list, it must possess *just one* of the following elements:

- Absence of the purported objectives of the activity or game
- Potential to embarrass a student in front of the rest of the class
- Focus on eliminating students from participation
- Overemphasis on and concern about the students having "fun"
- Lack of emphasis on teaching motor skills and lifetime physical fitness skills
- Extremely low participation time factors
- Extremely high likelihood for danger, injury, and harm

Can you think of a game that does not qualify? The "potential to embarrass" could stop just about any physical activity or game during adolescence! According to Williams, dodgeball is a "target" sport where kids are eliminated from competition and potentially face embarrassment and emotional scarring.

This focus on reducing activities that lead to dangerous behavior has prompted schools to ban other potentially harmful actions such as passing out birthday party invitations, touching of any kind, use of soccer or footballs on the playground, and eating treats made by someone other than your own parent. These are just a few examples of how an incident or two turns into a complete exclusion of an activity. Instead of teaching children how to lose or deal with not getting invited to a birthday party, society is choosing to protect children from such "hardships."

Without a doubt, children can be cruel to one another, and this will happen whether dodgeball is a part of PE curricula or not. Instead of focusing on removing every possible obstacle or embarrassment, successful families focus on helping children be strong in their own skin and self-assured in their abilities. They focus on building emotionally balanced children that understand they are not always going to win, there will always be bullies, and life is full of challenges.

Emotional balance is our ability to control, manage, and express our emotions. Research began to surface in the 1990s, when psychologists Daniel Goleman, Peter Salovey, John Mayer, and others released information on the subject of emotional intelligence. Because of their exploration, many believe emotional self-regulation is more important than a high IQ today. When we witness people with great intelligence flounder while others of a lesser IQ succeed, the difference can often be explained by how the latter manages their emotional self. The five key areas of this new intelligence are:

- **Knowing one's emotions**—Recognizing a feeling as it happens can give people a greater certainty about their feelings, often leading to better decision-making skills.

- **Managing emotions**—The ability to handle feelings so they are appropriate builds upon self-awareness. Those that excel in managing emotions can bounce back quickly from setbacks.

- **Motivating oneself**—People that can channel their emotions in the service of a goal can better motivate themselves to achieve outstanding performance.

- **Recognizing emotions in others**—People that demonstrate empathy are more attuned to subtle social signals that indicate what others may need or want.

- **Handling relationships**—The skill to manage emotions in others is the basis of the art of relationships. This ability can enhance popularity, leadership, and interpersonal effectiveness.

Helping your children better understand their feelings and how to use them is a highly effective use of your time as a parent. Emotional balance is a skill that greatly complements a driven child as they move up the ladder of success.

The Science of Balancing the Brain

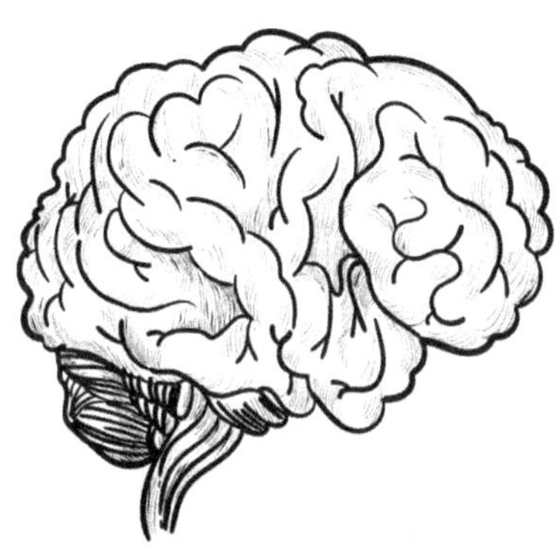

For decades, there have been varying hypotheses as to why people learn and think so differently. However, neuroscience is beginning to help us understand how we interpret and react to information and the various regions of the brain that can be developed through our unique experiences.

Traditionally and for simplicity, the brain has two distinct sides—the left and right. The left side of the brain is responsible for logic and organization. It thrives on order and sequence and focuses on text instead of context. People that access their left brain have a high level of organizational skills and common-sense logic and naturally tend to have views that are more black and white. Many accountants, engineers, and statisticians are "left-brained."

The right brain, however, is responsible for emotions, non-verbal cues, and context. We commonly get that "gut" or "loving" feeling from this side of the brain. Those that are seen as right-brained typically have a high level of creativity, are capable of abstract thinking, and see things in different shades of grey. Artists, musicians, and those in marketing are typically more "right-brained."

Aside from the left and right side, however, are the top and the bottom regions of the brain. The bottom brain, or brain stem, is responsible for our most primal actions, such as survival skills and split-second decisions. The amygdala is a very important, almond-shaped mass that resides in this lower region. Its main function is to process memories, decision making, and emotional reactions. The amygdala is your internal security system and has the power to completely take over your brain when it feels threatened.

For example, when your child unexpectedly throws a ball in your direction, the amygdala makes sure you lift your hands up and turn away to protect yourself. It doesn't take the time to think about all of the possible outcomes of the ball hitting you in the head nor does it move each body part separately; it just reacts. These unconscious reactions are very important for safety but can also create emotional imbalances if not integrated with the upstairs brain.

The top brain, or cortex, helps you connect ideas and develop relationships with others. It is responsible for your conscious thoughts and allows you to make ethical and moral decisions. One important fact about the upstairs brain is that it is not fully developed until your 20s. So it is perfectly natural for your child to have illogical reasons why he spray painted the dog's tail, colored the refrigerator to make it "pretty," or used air freshener as hairspray.

Building a balanced child means integrating these basic regions of the brain. One significant discovery is that our life experiences are largely responsible for this balance and integration. This would explain why many therapy sessions start with a family history. Growing up in a positive or negative environment can truly impact your emotional self.

During an experience, our brain cells or neurons activate and form connections with other neurons, developing an expansive web inside our head. If you hear the sound of a train, you can picture a train you have seen in the past. That simple sound can bring to your conscious mind very vivid experiences from many years ago. You may not have thought about trains for a long time, but the memory was stored in your filing system. You just needed a catalyst to bring it out of storage. Our brains have around one hundred billion of these neurons, each with an average of ten thousand connections.

The science of neuroplasticity directly relates to our ability to improve emotional balance. It refers to our ability to change or rewire our brains by deliberately creating new neurological connections and pathways. This means our brain continues to change throughout our life. If we make positive changes in our thought patterns, we can become more positive, but the opposite can also be true. Knowing this as a parent, however, is of great importance because changing your brain as an adult is not an easy process. If you can help your children build a positive web of neurons from an early age, it is more likely to stick with them throughout adulthood.

This malleability of the brain is most notable in one particular study involving London cab drivers. The streets of London, England, are known for their lack of organization and patterns that make them difficult to navigate and memorize. Brain images of local drivers with varying levels of experience were taken. The result? The images showed above-average growth of the hippocampus—the part of the brain corresponding to spatial intelligence. The more experienced the driver, the larger the section of the brain.

While this information may seem overwhelming as a parent, understand that your child's brain will naturally develop under normal family circumstances. But given this new wealth of information, parents can better shape the balance of their child's brain without being at the mercy of chance. And it can actually start as early as birth.

Building Emotional Balance

It Starts on Day One

Building emotional balance begins in infancy. From the moment a child is brought into this world and placed in his or her parents' arms, they are learning. A parent's emotional state (their ability to control their emotions as well as empathize and sympathize) can positively or negatively impact a newborn child's emotional state.

As the nervous system is being built, parents can have a tremendous influence in helping their child learn to regulate emotions by being a calming influence and building a strong bond. Research notes that children that are able to better recover from emotional states at the ages of seven and eight have "high vagal tone," which relates to the ability to regulate the involuntary physiological processes of the autonomic nervous system—the system of the body under construction during infancy. This system allows children to more effectively soothe and calm themselves after a stressful situation.

Children that do not form a secure attachment to one or both parents are often found to be more aggressive, defiant, and hyperactive when they are older. Parents that respond inconsistently to an infant's needs or negatively interfere with the child's activities are also more likely to produce children that explore less, cry often, and are more anxious. Simply put, infants cry to express discomfort, stress, or fear. Parents that neglect these responses allow their child to experience more discomfort, stress, or fear.

The first year is the most important time to build this emotional system. It starts with your ability to communicate with your child nonverbally by mimicking emotional cues and showing empathy when your child cries. In infancy, a child's cry typically means one of three things: They are hungry, they need a diaper change, or they are tired. After solving the issue, parents should linger for a positive interaction. This can greatly improve recovery time from stress. The positive interaction tells the child, "That experience was uncomfortable, but now everything is okay." You start to plant the seeds of emotional balance.

Connect First, Solve Problems Second

Adults often see a child's problems as trivial, but those that respond with empathy can further help the process of integrating their child's brain and preventing outbursts from further escalation. Your child's feelings are important to them at the time, and when you deny those negative feelings, it can actually intensify the effect. How do you feel when someone dismisses your feelings?

Responding with comments such as "Don't be angry" or "You shouldn't be sad" conveys that it is not normal to have these feelings. The effect of this response could lead to a right brain that never seeks the consoling logic of the left. When an emotion is acknowledged first, the left brain can begin to heal the negativity. Don't try to suppress negative feelings; help your children better manage them.

Inevitably, you will experience a full-blown tantrum that seemingly comes from out of nowhere. Daniel Siegel, author and clinical professor at the UCLA School of Medicine, summarizes this occurrence as "flipping our lid" when a child loses any ability to reason and explodes emotionally. Logic is tossed aside as the aforementioned amygdala literally shuts down access to the more rational upstairs brain. Science suggests connecting with your child emotionally can begin to disarm the security system and allow the conscious brain to offer its healing power.

I-Message Is Not a Smartphone App

Haim Ginott, author of the renowned book *Between Parent and Child*, was one of the first to study I-messages. He found framing sentences in a way that expresses how you are feeling because of someone's actions is more likely to gain understanding. When you tell someone how you feel, it is difficult for them to argue because it is how *you* feel. Conversely, if you frame the problem in a way that puts the blame on the other person, you will likely get a defensive or argumentative reaction. Parents that use I-messages have reported a higher likelihood of changing behavior, preserving self-esteem, and protecting the parent-child relationship.

Most parents at some point will deal with the dreaded "I hate you!" from their child. Your initial reactions may be "You shouldn't say that!" or, even worse, "I hate you too!" but consider the effectiveness of those statements. The first does not explain why the phrase is wrong, and the second proves it is okay to say. An I-message would sound more like this: "I know you are angry that you cannot watch more television, but when you say that you hate me, it makes me sad. I love you very much, and we have a lot of fun together, but it is now time to do your homework like we discussed." Describing how a child's behavior affected you negatively instead of telling them how they should feel or act can have a profound effect on your child's ability to empathize and change behavior.

Storytelling

A father is helping his daughter learn how to ride a bike without training wheels. "You ready, Sadie?" the father asks. "Ready!" Sadie replies, holding on to the handlebars.

"Okay, start pedaling!" the father calls, holding on to the back of the seat. Sadie starts to pedal, gaining her balance along the way. Seeing progress, her father lets go of the bike.

A few seconds pass before she realizes Daddy is not next to her anymore. She turns her head to see her father smiling and cheering from ten yards back. Her confidence wanes; she starts to wobble, falls off the bike, and scrapes her knee.

Her dad rushes to her side.

"You're okay, sweetie," her father consoles. "You were doing really well! Let's get back on and try it again."

"No!" Sadie cries, hugging her knees. "I don't want to ride bikes ever again!"

How can Sadie's father help her recover from this seemingly traumatic experience? Psychologists have used storytelling for years to help people get over emotionally-scarring incidents. Storytelling requires the brain to put together facts in an organized sequence, thus activating the logical side of the brain and connecting to the harmful emotion. The more times the story is told with the ending put into logical perspective, the less emotionally-charged it becomes.

When the initial shock of the experience fades, Sadie's father asks her to tell him the story of what happened. Sadie recalls the events using left-brained sequencing and logic.

"And then I looked back, and you were gone," she says.

"That must have been pretty scary," her father suggests. "But it looks like you are feeling better, right?"

"Yes," she replies.

"You were doing such a great job. Why don't you get back on the bike, and this time, I won't let go until you tell me to. Okay?"

Now that Sadie is calm and able to discuss what happened, she can put the incident into perspective and know that it was an accident. Recalling the story of a traumatic event tends to "cool" the emotional side of the brain.

For a younger child, you may have to recall most of the story, allowing your child to interject with facts whenever possible. Writing the story down and drawing pictures of the incident can also help the healing process if talking is not easy. Different experiences can have varying degrees of healing time, so be patient. You may also find that your child has an easier time opening up when involved in another activity like playing a board game or coloring instead of a planned interrogation.

Name That Emotion

Emotional balance is not about reducing the emotions we experience but being able to better *understand* our emotions. Putting feelings into words has long been a psychological tool to help people overcome trauma, but up until the last decade, we really did not know why.

Matthew Lieberman, psychology professor at UCLA, led a team in a brain imaging study to find out how this process works. They discovered that when subjects were able to correctly label their emotions, it reduced the activity in the amygdala by activating the right ventrolateral prefrontal cortex–the area of the brain most known for vigilance and discrimination. This exercise thus forces the use of the left brain, lessening the emotional impact and allowing the individual to better cope and react.

Expanding your child's vocabulary and helping them understand proper responses to these stimuli can go a long way in building emotional balance. Using more descriptive words or phrases when pointing out your child's emotions can better help them decipher their true feelings. For example:

1. "You look happy after your snack."

2. "You seem angry at me. Did I do something to hurt your feelings?"

3. "I understand you are jealous that your sister got presents for her birthday."

As you are reading a book or watching television with your child, you can point out certain characters and ask how they might be feeling in certain situations: "He lost his ball. How do you think he feels?" or "She found a present on her doorstep. What emotion is she feeling?" Role playing different emotions can also be an effective way for a child to internalize how they respond to different situations. Here is a list of other emotions to expand vocabulary:

APATHY	Betrayed	Doubt
Demoralized	Blue	Dread
Discouraged	Disappointed	Embarrassed
Forgetful	Heartbroken	Horrified
Giving up	Hurt	Hysterical
Hardened	Inadequate	Irrational
Inattentive	Melancholy	Nervous
Indecisive	Misunderstood	Paranoid
Indifferent	Mourning	Scared
Unfocused	Remorse	Secretive
Useless	Sadness	Superstitious
Vague	Vulnerable	Suspicious
	Wounded	Tense
GRIEF		Timid
Anguished	**FEAR**	Uneasy
Ashamed	Anxious	Worry

LUST
Compulsive
Craving
Envy
Exploitative
Fixated
Gluttonous
Greedy
Impatient
Pushy

ANGER
Abrasive
Aggressive
Belligerent
Demanding
Destructive
Furious
Hostility
Impatience
Irate
Rage
Savage
Stewing
Sullen

PRIDE
Boastful
Conceited
Critical
Disdain
Gloating
Haughty
Hypocritical
Judgmental
Prejudiced
Vain

COURAGE
Adventurous
Confident
Creative
Daring
Decisive
Eager
Enthusiastic
Flexible
Motivated
Open
Self-sufficient
Visionary
Willing

ACCEPTANCE
Appreciative
Balance
Compassion
Considerate
Empathy
Friendly
Gracious
Joyful
Loving
Tender
Understanding
Warm

PEACE
Calm
Centered
Oneness
Serenity
Tranquility

Just Press "Pause"

As your children expand their emotional vocabulary and understand the bodily responses from negative feelings, they can then begin to control the reaction to these responses. Helping your children come up with positive ways to handle big emotions like anger and sadness before they get the best of them can drastically reduce future occurrences.

When an outburst has occurred and the dust has settled, talk to your child about ways it could have been avoided. Brainstorm ways to control strong, harmful emotions before they turn into action, such as taking a deep breath, counting to 10, or using a keyword such as "pause." The pause button on a remote control is a great visual way to help children interrupt a quick emotional response and take a moment for rational contemplation. It is also an easy way for parents to quickly communicate to their children before the response becomes an issue.

Many families use "pause" regularly when they feel another member is starting to lose control. Consistent repetition is the key to teaching your children how to "press pause" before they react inappropriately. It is an important trigger to activate the left brain and rational contemplation. You will know it is working when they start telling *you* to "pause"!

Bedtime Positivity

Rick Hanson, Ph.D., a neuropsychologist and author of *Hardwiring Happiness*, supports studies of the amygdala, noting that while it does respond to positive events and feelings, it is predisposed to focus more on negative events. This primal system helped keep the Cro-Magnum man safe from danger, but the life of a caveman was much different from life today. Back then, much of the day was spent in the wild fighting to protect territory and hunting for food. The amygdala kept him aware of any possible dangers to literally save his life. Today, I hunt for food at the grocery store and set the alarm at night to keep my family safe.

Over time, this primitive focus on negative experiences can build up in our brain and cause greater sensitivity and reaction. The more intense the experience, the more likely our brain stores the information. Most adults remember where they were on September 11, 2001, when terrorists attacked the United States. They remember what they were doing, how they found out, and what they felt when they witnessed planes crashing into the World Trade Center. Even now, people can recount the event as though it was yesterday.

Negative situations stick with us because they tend to be more vivid in our minds. They can begin to consume us as negativity breeds more negativity. We witness this in the media. Ever notice how much of the evening news focuses on adverse events? Which house burned down last night? Who was murdered? What now causes cancer?

Battling this negativity bias by helping children seek and recall positive experiences can do wonders for their emotional health. Hanson argues that people begin to thrive when the ratio of positive moments to negative reaches 3:1 and, ideally, higher. Bedtime is a perfect opportunity to share the positive memories of the day. Ask your child, "What was your favorite part of today?" Help them expand upon their stories and assess how they felt in each moment. It can assist in building a healthy mindset and send them off to sleep with happy thoughts.

Use the Force

In the original Star Wars movie, Jedi Master Obi-Wan Kenobi describes the Force as an energy field created by all living things that binds the galaxy together. Throughout the series, characters exhibit various powers, both good and evil. The Force naturally enhanced mental and physical capabilities when characters such as Luke Skywalker found himself in a dangerous circumstance. While telekinesis or levitation may not be on our list of talents down here on Earth, we do have ways to utilize energy from our body during stressful situations.

One such use of this phenomenon is channeling the energy of the "butterflies." If you have ever gotten that nervous feeling in the pit of your stomach before a presentation, you know how easily it can cripple your performance. The "butterflies," which is actually a rush of adrenaline, can kick the logical side of your brain into overdrive: "What if I stutter too much? What if I lose my place and cannot recover? What if...?" These nerves can create a detrimental flight response inside your head. We spend a lot of time finding remedies to rid ourselves of this difficult anxiety, when in reality, it is impossible to do.

Athletes, musicians, and presenters often admit to getting nervous regardless of how many times they practice or perform. Younger children can often mistake these nerves for a stomachache or illness. Because of this, they begin to think of this pressure as a negative force and try to resist it. You can shift this mindset to a positive response by understanding the true purpose of adrenaline. The extra energy is being produced to help your performance under stress. Adrenaline wants you to succeed!

By teaching your child to embrace these feelings instead of suppressing them, they can reduce anxiety and feel more at ease when trying something new, performing in front of an audience, and taking calculated risks. As a parent, try to think ahead and help your child prepare to understand the pressure they may feel in certain situations. Consistent mindfulness and positivity will give them emotional tools to embrace the nerves it takes to stand out in front of the crowd.

If It Takes a Village...

Adolescence is a time for your child to begin to understand who they are and separate from you. Almost at the flip of a switch you go from "hero" to "zero" in your child's eyes, and although disheartening, it is a completely normal process. If handled correctly, it shall pass.

This can leave parents feeling somewhat helpless however, as it becomes difficult to control a child's social circle and whereabouts. As the fight for independence begins, it is important that you surround your family with people that share similar values as you. If it takes a village to raise a child, then you should take the time to find the right village!

Do your children have a community that they can lean on for emotional support? Are there mentors, groups, or activities that can help your children learn and experience new things? Your opinion as a parent may become "uncool," but if your children have access to other adults that share in your vision, they can continue to grow in the manner you hope. Communicate with teachers, coaches, religious leaders, etc., to ensure they are getting the counseling they need outside of the home.

Building great relationships with other parents is also a great way to stay connected and ensure your child's development. Overwhelmingly, research has found children that are consistently monitored by their parents in relation to their friends, activities, and whereabouts are less likely to participate in troublesome behavior such as alcohol/drug use, criminal activity, and sexual promiscuity. A good village allows your children to find independence but also helps you identify any troubling signs along the way *without* becoming overbearing.

Put on Your Poker Face

The poker face has long been a staple in the card-playing community as a way of disguising your emotions and bodily reactions to keep players from reading you. Many parents wish for their child to be honest with them, yet few take the time to understand just what they might hear. If you want open, honest communication, then be prepared for discussions about sex, alcohol, drugs, bullying, and other teenage issues. This is not easy.

Parents with teenage or adult children should now take on the role of consultant. Ask yourself, what type of person would I want consulting me? Would you want someone that overreacts and scrutinizes your every misstep? Of course not! And your children feel the same way.

Parents say they want to hear what goes on in their child's life, but then overreact or punish when it happens. What are the odds they open up again? Be prepared to hit your own pause button and listen carefully without interjecting with answers and opinions right away.

We all experienced adolescence. It can be an emotionally confusing, complex, and difficult time as a child sorts out who they are. Be mindful that your reactions will make or break your ability to be a part of your child's life. React with compassion and understanding, and be grateful your adolescent is willing to talk to you!

CHAPTER THREE

CREATIVITY

As children, we were constantly told to use our imaginations—especially when we complained about being bored. These days, however, the need for this mental exercise is vanishing as technology such as video games, television, and the internet provide an unlimited amount of mindless entertainment. Many school educators would also point to the increasing importance of standardized test scores as the corrupter of creativity. Teachers must focus on increasing grades rather than the process of learning and creative problem solving.

In 2010 educational psychology professor Kyung Hee Kim analyzed the creativity of 300,000 American children and adults using a measure known as Torrance Tests of Creative Thinking (TTCT). This test measures creative potential in areas such as art, literature, science, mathematics, architecture, engineering, business, leadership, and inter-personal relationships. While Kyung's results suggest creativity overall has diminished in the last 20 years, the most significant decrease was found in children in kindergarten through third grade.

In another study of 1,500 children, ranging in ages from three to five, 98 percent were found to be "geniuses" in divergent thinking. But by age thirteen, the figure was a disappointing 10 percent. Reasons for the freefall presented in these studies include schools focusing on test scores and memorization, the fear of failure, and pressure to be "normal" or "cool."

Parents are also putting pressure on test scores and GPAs. If children get good grades, their futures will be more secure. They will get into great colleges and later, land well-paying jobs. Memorizing and regurgitating information is seemingly the road to success. Not to say grades are not important but many of the most prosperous individuals are doing what others are not and nurturing the creative mind.

True, creativity is not necessary for academic success. In fact, the creative trait has shown to be distinctly different from the basic definition of intelligence. Yet in a study performed by IBM, creativity was the characteristic rated most important in a leader—beating out rigor, management discipline, integrity, or even vision. The leaders considered creative tend to be more confident in taking on new challenges because they are able to think of new, exciting solutions and cope with setbacks in a more constructive way. They understand that failure is a part of the process.

Companies like Google and Apple have quickly become masters of innovation as they open their company architecture for ideas to flow freely and without fear of failure. This lack of structure, focus on individualism, and notion that there are no bad ideas has pushed these companies straight to the top of the Fortune 500.

Like these companies, successful families focus on creativity in much the same way. While it may seem that a group of individuals thinking in the same manner would be ideal, creating an atmosphere where each member has a voice and individuality is a must in building a family legacy. This diversification of thoughts and talents helps families safeguard from wealth destruction and adapt to changing environments. The good news is neither you nor your children need to have a "creative gene" to be innovative, but you must understand how creativity is cultivated.

What Is Creativity?

Creativity is often associated with the entertainment and art industries. The ability to paint, perform, make music, or build something from scratch most often gets the attention of the media. And while creativity does encompass these activities, it is also not limited to them.

*Creativity is the ability to solve problems
when there are no easy solutions.*

The primary objective of creativity is *idea* creation. As the aforementioned studies suggest, young children are great at being creative initially. They have little experience and constraints; thus they can have the craziest ideas and uninhibited imaginations.

When I was a kid, I remember being at my friend's house, trying to start a fire by rubbing two sticks together. We got the idea from a television program we watched earlier that week. It was a cold morning, and we had been rubbing the sticks together for what felt like hours. The sticks became warm from the friction but no fire. Eventually, a little water dripped onto the sticks, and we saw smoke! We were close! We ran into the house to get more hot water hoping it would continue to heat the sticks. We were oblivious to the true elements needed to start a fire, but we kept trying.

Would I call this a failed experiment? No. Sure, we never got so much as a spark, but we learned water will not start a fire and also stumbled upon the properties of steam.

Most importantly, however, we practiced the trial-and-error method. Today you can easily search the internet for "how to start a fire," but it is the process of experimentation that will enhance your child's creativity.

Thomas Edison is most noted for important innovations that changed our society, such as the phonograph, the motion-picture camera, and the light bulb; he actually had over 1,000 patents in the United States alone. He was a great idea generator, but despite his accomplishments, many of his thoughts never saw the light of day. "I have not failed," he said. "I've just found ten thousand ways that won't work." If anything, those failures pushed him to achieve the great inventions we now use everyday. If, however, he quit after the first or second failure, what would life be like today?

The Creative Process

"I just wasn't born with the 'creative gene'" is a common lament of people that believe they do not have an innate predisposition to creativity. But like so many things in life, creativity can be *learned* and is in unlimited supply. You just need to know how to develop it.

A leading expert in creativity, Dr. Keith Sawyer, describes the creative process as having eight key steps:

1. Ask

In order to get the proverbial "juices flowing," you have to ask the right question. Nobel Prize–winning theoretical physicist Albert Einstein once said, "The formulation of a problem is often more essential than its solution." Creativity begins with asking a great question. While the entire process can be messy, this step can keep you focused on finding a solution.

2. Learn

Learning is a lifelong process. It is difficult to be creative without first having advanced knowledge of a particular topic. Would you be able to write a song with no experience in music? A musician needs to have a vast understanding of music notes, song construction, and instruments before the next great song hits the charts.

3. Look

Creativity is boosted by being observant and exposing yourself to new stimuli and experiences. Rodolfo Llinas, a neuroscientist at NYU School of Medicine, estimates that only 20 percent of our perceptions are based on actual information from the outside world. This leaves 80 percent to be imagined by our brain. Have you ever tried to recall a story with your spouse or friend and each of you have very different versions? By actively being present or in the moment, you may discover new observations initially missed at first glance.

4. Play

Unstructured play is a key to our children exploring the world. A simple cardboard refrigerator box can become a world of wonder to a young mind. However, fear of judgment causes us to become more conservative and timid as we age. Finding time to "tinker" or experience something new can lead to exciting discoveries for any age group.

5. Think

Creativity is a numbers game. Like Thomas Edison, most of your ideas will likely never turn into genius, but it takes the uninhibited approach and understanding of failure to be innovative. Pablo Picasso produced 20,000 pieces of art. Albert Einstein wrote more than 240 scientific papers. Richard Branson started 250 companies. All of these people are known for only a few successes, but it was the quantity of ideas that led them to eventually finding fame and fortune.

6. Fuse

Combining different ideas often leads to exciting new revelations. Fuse together peanut butter and chocolate and the Reese's Peanut Butter Cup is born. Add the internet and shopping and you get Amazon.com. Neuroscience research has found combining two separate ideas leads to greater brain activity where problem solving and higher thought take place. Thus, the practice of fusion could lead to greater problem solving skills and the openness needed for creativity to transpire.

7. Choose

The "Aha! Moment"—the point in time when a possible solution rushes through your mind. Have you ever woken up in the middle of the night with the answer to a question? Or thought of a solution to a problem while running on the treadmill? Creativity's needed sidekick is logic. As ideas are generated, they must be examined to see if they are relevant. Your best ideas must be put through a critical process to determine if they fulfill the question and follow any guidelines set forth. Take the creative thought, and now put it into real-world application.

8. Make

Now it is time to actually build the prototype. Turning creativity into a tangible item quickly is important in today's fast-paced world. It is now time to get your hands dirty and take action. Not to mention, as you begin the building process, you will likely come across better ideas and evolutions of your original thought.

As Sawyer notes, you might not need or use all of the steps above, nor will they necessarily happen in that exact order. Creativity is understood to be a messy process, but by learning and practicing these steps, you and your children will have an arsenal of tools to become creative innovators.

Building Creativity

Create a Problem

While creativity is often thought as being "outside of the box," most great innovations begin with constraints. Like a menu at a restaurant, if you are given too many options, it is difficult to make decisions. Creativity is greatly enhanced by formulating specific questions and constructing parameters from which to create.

For example, during craft time, pose a problem to your children and have them create a solution with random items available. Let's say you want to build a birdhouse with different objects around the house, such as Legos, pipe-cleaners, wooden dowels, and a potato. Using Sawyer's eight creative steps, you may first have them compile a list of components of a birdhouse: enclosure, seed dispenser, and perch. Find pictures of birdhouses to aid in the research. From there, start to play and build.

This type of creative thinking may also help when your child has a problem in their personal life. Perhaps they are invited to two birthday parties on the same day at the same time. Your child does not want to hurt either friend. You might be quick to offer your opinion, but instead, help them formulate the question: "How can I celebrate both birthdays while being attentive to my friends' feelings?" Then your child can create a list of possible solutions and discuss the pros and cons of each. Practicing this process is the key to developing more creative problem-solvers.

Free Play

Creativity is nurtured by freedom. Parents do not need to schedule every waking hour. Free play allows children to make their own fun and explore things that excite them. As a kid, my friends and I would play outside until the bell rang for dinner. We did not need parental involvement. Children need to learn how to combat their boredom. Video games, the internet, and social media are easy answers to this, but they do little to inspire creativity.

Since 1950 children's free play has declined and childhood mental disorders have been on the rise. This is not due to newly discovered disorders that were previously overlooked; the clinical questionnaires for assessing anxiety and depression have not changed in over sixty years. Studies show the decline in free play has decreased empathy and increased narcissism in children. When children play freely, they often enter pretend worlds and act like adults. Playing "house" can help children develop social skills and empathy as they act out different scenarios. You must pretend to be someone else thus, giving an insight into how others might think, feel, and act.

In her book, *Pretend Play in Childhood: Foundation of Adult Creativity*, psychologist Sandra Russ states that unstructured free play builds a foundation of creativity that lasts through adulthood. Exploring and trying new activities develops cognitive processing that will be needed when children grow up. Having a broad range of experiences can be great for problem solving and can also help them find what may eventually be an exciting life path.

The Tinkering Zone

There should be a place in your home that is specifically set aside for "tinkering." As a child, my father's work bench in the basement was a great place for me to build, learn, and create. It was filled with tools, wood scraps, and other interesting household objects. When I was six years old, my grandfather passed away. I witnessed my grandmother's sadness and desperately wanted to cheer her up. I spent days in that cold, damp basement trying to build the perfect gift. I hammered some 2x4s into a cluster of wood that somewhat resembled an airplane, although that was not by design.... I painted it with six coats of green paint. I wanted it to be perfect!

My grandmother was so touched by the sentiment that she immediately hung it on the wall next to her favorite chair. For the next 25 years and up until the day she passed away, that "thing" never left her sight. It became a great story we shared as I grew up and a memento of my love for her. It wasn't the beauty of my artwork but the time and effort that touched her most. It never would have happened without that area in our home.

Don't like the idea of your child playing with hammers, nails, and saws? I understand. Have a craft area with supplies ready for when the mood or boredom strikes. Paper, crayons, markers, glue, glitter—the possibilities are endless. It doesn't have to be expensive or extraordinary. Many of these supplies can be found at the dollar store or even lying around your home.

Taking apart and dissecting old mechanical items or electronics can also be a fun and intriguing "tinkering" experiment. Exploring the inner workings of an old radio or computer can enhance creativity and the understanding of how things work. Just make sure your child knows what is available for tinkering so you don't find your new tablet in pieces!

Creative Games

You also do not need to buy elaborate games to be creative! Simple mental exercises can be done anywhere.

Car rides— even short ones to the grocery store—can be a great time to get your children thinking. Use the fusion technique and ask your children what they would get if they combined two completely random objects, such as an iPad and an orange. What purpose could it serve? Perhaps you could have an iPad that smells like fresh oranges or an edible iPad for when it eventually crashes and cannot be repaired. The actual real-world application is less important than simply the process of generating fun ideas.

Another fusion activity involves combining two random words to form a company name. Have your children then decide the company's purpose and create a logo. Use random word generator websites to help spark the exercise. How would "Runway Bandage Inc." change the world?

Aside from fusing ideas together, you can also subtract, divide, or multiply an object. Try subtracting or removing a component to see how it might work. Can the object still complete its purpose? Does the newly created object have another feature or perform more efficiently now? It may seem ludicrous to take parts away from an already well-performing mechanism, but Steve Jobs created Apple Computers by trying to simplify his PC and debug its software. For example, an Apple computer mouse only has one button compared to the standard two-button PC mouse.

Dividing an object allows you to break up something complex into many simple parts. I embarked upon another wayward project as a child—disassembling my mother's purple, 10-speed bicycle. I observed how the braking system, pedals, and gears all worked individually, which helped me learn how to better repair and maintain my bike. It also taught me the importance of tracking how the pieces fit back together! Sorry, Mom! Division allows an opportunity to perhaps improve a smaller component to improve the entire object. How could you make the pedals more comfortable or improve the braking system to decrease stopping distance?

The multiplication method of creativity involves taking a certain component of an object and doubling (or tripling) an attribute of it. For example, if I were to take the gear from the bike I disassembled and doubled its size, would it make it easier or harder to pedal? Would it help me go faster? The answer has already been answered as we have multi-gear bikes, but actually working through the process to come up with the same answer is a great experiment for children!

Be in the Moment

An important aspect of creativity is being in the moment. Often as we build competencies in certain tasks or go about our day, we have the tendency to let our minds wander or "zone out." Sometimes while driving to my office in the morning, I have to think if I actually brushed my teeth. My routine has become so automatic that I can turn my attention to other things while getting ready for the day. But when this occurs, you lose the ability to improve the process. Going through the motions is not an effective creative practice but keeping an extra tooth brush in your desk is highly recommended just in case.

Another example is the guitarist that has played a song so many times that he can play it perfectly without a thought. To improve the song however, he must make a conscious effort to change the arrangement, tempo, or key. Even if these changes do not make the song better, he may discover something to help him write the next one.

Being in the moment, especially during mindless activities, is a great way to inspire creativity and improve our way of life. Encourage your children to maximize the moment and find little ways to change the day, practice session, or playtime to keep it from getting stale.

Being attentive to your surroundings is also a great way to seek inspiration. New Zealand pop sensation Lorde wrote her first chart-topping hit "Royals" after seeing a picture of former baseball star George Brett signing baseballs in *National Geographic*. He was wearing a Kansas City Royals jersey, and from that one fascinating word, she was able to create a hit (no pun intended). "It was just that word. It's really cool," she told *VH1*.

Help your children better notice their surroundings. Ask them to point out an item in the doctor's waiting room they have never noticed before. Play "I Spy" or go people-watching in the park. Practice ways to focus attention throughout the day. Inspiration could be where you least expect it.

Make Time for Downtime

While being active and social are important, downtime and sleep are an absolute necessity to foster creativity. Experts report that people that get a goodnight's rest are 33% more creative than those that do not. You must give your brain time to connect ideas and answer questions you have posed. By taking your conscious mind off the project, it allows your brain to expand its web and create the "Ah Ha" moment.

Studies in neuroscience show your brain is just as active when sleeping as awake and sometimes even more so. After you learn something, your brain goes to work storing the information and finding links to previous memories. It then reorganizes the information, paving the way to better insight. Additionally, during certain phases of sleep, the brain becomes more active if the person has learned something new that day. Turns out the old phrase "just sleep on it" rings true.

During the *Sleep Inspires Insight* study, participants were given a series of eight digits and with two rules, were asked to find the ninth digit in the series. The participants were unaware that there was an underlying short-cut to completing the puzzle. They were taught the longer strategy using three examples and then given an eight-hour break. One group slept, another was asked to stay awake during the day, and the last group was asked to stay awake at night. Subsequently, the subjects were then asked to complete ten more sequences. Sleep more than doubled the probability of figuring out the hidden rule compared to the other two groups.

Learning followed by sleep allows the information you have gathered to become clearer and enables you to find better solutions to problems. This practice may help your children when they have a difficult time grasping a concept or studying for an upcoming test. Learn the topic, and then let your brain do the work. If nothing else, it is a great excuse to take a nap!

CHAPTER FOUR

INFLUENCE

Throughout life, we are shaped by many external forces. The company we keep and our experiences influence our thoughts, actions, and perceptions of the world around us. We can point to people that have had a positive influence in our lives and people that have negatively affected us. Regardless, influence is a part of everyday life.

Oprah Winfrey, named *Forbes' Magazine*'s Most Influential Celebrity of 2013, was raised in a rural, poverty-stricken area of Mississippi. No one would have thought that she would eventually become a household name. But through her television show, book club, and philanthropy, she has influenced many aspects of our culture. Her focus is not only helping people help themselves but influencing others to help their communities. She has helped women and men, young and old, feel empowered all over the globe. But what is it that makes her so influential?

Oprah's influence is not a result of a single action. She cultivates her influence in different ways. She appeals to the *head, heart, and hand*:

- Head: Rational Appeal
  The Oprah Winfrey Show aired from 1986 to 2011 and during that span was nominated for 86 awards, winning 64 times. Since retiring from her show, she started the television network OWN and at the age of 60, has a net worth just shy of three billion dollars. For rational appeal, it is necessary to prove why people should follow you. Oprah's vast resume of accomplishments gives her the ability to influence her audience.

- Heart: Emotional Appeal
  Avid watchers of *The Oprah Winfrey Show* often cite her openness and willingness to show her human side as one of her most appealing traits. Her struggle with weight gain and body image, for example, was highly publicized throughout her career and helped her connect with a majority of woman in the audience. Everyone witnessed her emotional highs and lows and

connected with her on a level difficult for many to achieve.

- Hand: Cooperative Appeal

  Oprah is a name synonymous with giving. Having donated millions of dollars to charity and her own foundations, she is seen as someone who truly cares about helping those that cannot help themselves. From signing a wooden dog bone to be auctioned at the Mississippi Animal Rescue League to giving 300 audience members $1,000 each to donate to the charity of their choice, she is able to influence through giving and lending a hand.

Influence vs. Leadership

Being influential does not necessarily mean the same as being a leader. A leader is often given authority to influence and can wield this power to motivate people. A manager, for example, can make an employee complete a task and threaten their job if they do not follow orders. An influential person, however, does not need this control. Oprah never had the authority to make her audience watch her show. It was her vast appeal that created such a large following. Thus, leadership is the tip of the iceberg; influence is the great mass underneath.

Not everyone wants to be a leader or has the capacity to lead. Yet research suggests that 85% of a person's success in business can be attributed to his or her ability to persuade and influence others. We have to influence people daily regardless of our career or station in life. A doctor has to influence patients to take their prescribed medication or start an exercise regimen. A financial advisor has to influence clients to invest when the stock market is down. A parent has to influence a child in so many ways! Your child does not need to be a leader, but their ability to positively influence others will be a driving force behind success.

Influence Is Fragile

Our lives are slowly becoming less and less private. With technology and social media, everything is out for the public to see. Hence, our ability to influence is increasingly delicate. Like a waiter carrying a large tray of dishes, one misstep and your reputation can come crashing down. How many times have we witnessed politicians or media personalities lose their once upstanding reputation when a video or sound bite was uploaded to YouTube or Facebook?

During his presidential campaign in 2012, Mitt Romney was secretly recorded during a $50,000-per-plate fundraising dinner. The GOP presidential candidate already had difficulty relating to the general public due to his "wealthy" lifestyle, and his comments on this particular evening added to the problem.

There are 47 percent of the people who will vote for the president no matter what. All right, there are 47 percent who are with him, who are dependent upon government, who believe that they are victims, who believe that government has a responsibility to care for them, who believe that they are entitled to health care, to food, to housing, to you name it. That, that's an entitlement. And the government should give it to them.

Before this recording was released, Romney's approval rating had reached the highest level of the election, putting a sizable gap between him and President Obama. Within days, Romney's rating plummeted below that of President Obama and never again returned to its peak. Just like that, a candid five-minute conversation undid many years of hard work as he would later lose the election.

What Is Influence?

Long ago, influence was often associated with manipulation, using trickery to help sell your product or get people to follow you. People would utilize tactics they learned from the used car salesman with the slicked-back hair and sneaky grin, explaining the high points of the lemon of a car he was trying to sell. This form of influence offered short-term monetary rewards but sacrificed relationships and trust. As people became more aware of these tricks, they eventually became ineffective.

Mark Goulston, author of *Real Influence*, states long-term influence involves a focus on the "Three R's": Results, Reputation, and Relationships.

Results

- Do you have an "I can" or "I can't" mentality?
- Do you go for a great outcome?
- Are you ambitious?
- Can you help others get results?

Reputation

- Do you tell the truth even if it is difficult?
- Do you stand for your beliefs when faced with adversity?
- When you give your word, do you follow through?
- Do you stand behind people even when they are struggling?
- Do you practice what you preach?

Relationships

- Are you a pleasure to be around or are you stoked in negativity?

- Do you sacrifice short-term results to earn trust and confidence?
- Are you empathetic?
- Can you communicate effectively? Publicly or one-on-one?

If influence is such an important trait to success, why are there so little resources for children to build proficiency? School inherently creates a self-centered attitude as students naturally worry about individual grades. However, in adulthood, we are often working for the betterment of others. We go to work to help our company. We shuttle our kids to soccer practice and piano lessons to help them be well-rounded. We sacrifice our own time to help our community or those in need.

Successful families are often influential in their communities and understand the importance of influence in pursuit of their goals. Success cannot be accomplished alone. By making it a priority for the next generations to learn the skills of influence, children are often seen as natural leaders and better thrive in social settings.

Building Influence

It's All in Your Head

Achieving great results is just as much about your state of mind as it is your skill or expertise. We often judge someone's personality by their appearance. In fact, the way you look and the way you move make up more than

80 percent of someone's first impression of you. Think of a friend with a lot of confidence. Think of the way he or she walks. Do they keep their head down? Are their shoulders hunched? No! They walk tall and straight, with their shoulders back and their heads up. They smile and exude grace and poise. People are more likely to be influenced by someone that is sure of themselves, and this starts in the mind.

Captain Jack Sands was piloting his aircraft in the Vietnam War when he was shot down and taken prisoner. He was detained for seven years in the Hanoi prison camp—the same prison camp where Senator John McCain was held. Captain Sands was placed in solitary confinement. He could do no physical activity, and personal encounters were limited and monitored. If many of us were subjected to this torture, we would not come back a sane person. But Captain Sands found a way.

Even though he could not participate in any physical activity, he could be free mentally. In his mind, he created a beautiful golf course. He thought of every single detail, down to the color of the flags. For seven years, Captain Sands played 18 holes of golf from his five-foot by five-foot cell. Before the captain went to war, he only played golf casually, shooting around 100. After seven years of perfect mental golf, Captain Sands saw a dramatic improvement on the scorecard.

When he finally made it back home, he played a round of golf, scoring a 74. For almost a decade, Captain

Sands had no physical activity, and yet he took over twenty strokes off his game. Behold the power of the mind!

You may be thinking, "I have no confidence! How can I *exude* something I do not have? How can I help my child be confident?" Take a page from Captain Sands: *imagine* yourself confident. What would you look like? How would you dress? How would you carry yourself? Athletes and entertainers often use this same mental imagery to improve their performance. Help your children learn how to visualize confidence and watch as they transform.

There are four keys to proper mental imagery:

- **Imagery Perspective**

  Try to imagine the scenario as vividly as possible. The internal perspective is imagining the situation as you would see it through your own eyes. The external perspective, by comparison, is seeing the situation like you are watching a movie of yourself. Research suggests both methods provide performance improvement, so use what feels comfortable. Whether it is giving a great speech or making the game-winning shot, be consistent in which perspective you use.

- **Control**

  When you first start the imagery process, you or your child might make mistakes as the video plays in the mind. Controlling the outcome is important to building confidence. If you make a mistake or start playing a negative video, say to yourself, "That's not me," and rewind until you get it right.

- **Multiple Senses**

  Improving performance is more than just seeing it in your mind. Try to incorporate as many senses as possible. If you are practicing the perfect golf shot in your mind like Captain Sands, can you feel the grip of the club in your hands? Feel the warmth of the sun and hear the birds chirping? Can you smell the freshly cut grass? The more vivid the experience, the more the mind believes what it sees.

- **Speed**

  Change the speed to ensure you use multiple senses. Start the visualization in slow motion. Slowing down allows you to focus on specific fundamentals or aspects of your performance you wish to improve. As your comfort level grows, speed up the imagery to real-time.

Rewarding Honesty

Bobby Jones was not only an exceptionally skilled golfer but exemplified honesty and integrity. During the first round of the 1925 U.S. Open, his shot on the 11th hole fell into the deep rough of an embankment. When he took his stance, the head of his club grazed the grass, causing a slight movement of the ball. He proceeded to take the shot but told his playing partner and the USGA official covering the match that he was going to call a penalty on himself.

Unable to be talked out of it, Jones stood by his decision. Before he signed his scorecard, officials again argued with Jones, saying there was no penalty. However, Jones insisted he violated Rule 18 (moving the ball at rest after address) and took a 77 instead of a 76. This score forced a playoff, which he eventually lost.

When sports writers and journalists praised him for his honesty, Jones commented, "You might as well praise me for not robbing banks." Jones' integrity might have cost him a win, but it showed the true spirit of sportsmanship. Because of this, the USGA's Sportsmanship Award is now referred to as "The Bob Jones Award."

Encouraging and rewarding honesty is not always easy as a parent. If your son breaks an expensive vase throwing a ball in the house and comes to you to confess, how would you respond? Would you commend him for being honest? Would you punish him for breaking the vase?

If you punish your child for being honest, what is the motivation for him to continue telling the truth? Honesty should be appreciated and always trump the wrongdoing. Your children are going to make mistakes. If they do not feel comfortable coming to you, it limits your ability to effectively parent and teach.

Instead of a punishment that has no relevance to the crime, such as spanking or timeout, help them figure out a way to make it right. Perhaps they forgo their allowance until the price of the vase is recouped or they do extra chores to work off the cost. Even the most inspiring people make mistakes, but it is those that take responsibility for their actions, like Bobby Jones, that command greater influence. Children are not born with a moral code. Parents must combat lying and develop honesty over time.

Who Are You Online?

Before a person meets you face to face, they can do a simple online search to learn just about everything they need to know. From your Facebook profile to your Twitter feed or your job history on LinkedIn, you are on the grid.

A recent study by CareerBuilder.com found two in five companies do a social media search on potential job candidates. Of those companies, 34% of employers found content on an applicant's social media page that caused them to not hire them. It was concluded that employers are looking for three key things when searching online:

Does this person present themselves professionally?

Is this person well-rounded?

What can we tell about this person's character from his/her online profile?

Do your social media pages reflect how you want to be perceived? What about your children (if they are on social media)? Do their profiles match how they want others to see them? I am often amazed what teenagers are willingly posting online these days. One mistake can be captured is milliseconds.

Remember, future employers, clients, and even future family (i.e., in-laws) will see this. Online profiles are quickly becoming the new resumé. Are you properly monitoring your children's online activity? Do their social media profiles enhance their reputation or detract from it? These questions have never been more important.

Stop Selling Girl Scout Cookies

I cannot tell you how many times I am stopped in the office or on my way into the grocery store by a parent asking me if I want to buy cookies or popcorn to support their child's team or troop. Meanwhile, their child is sitting behind them, completely uninterested or, worse yet, not even there! Reaching a popcorn or cookie goal seems more important to some parents than teaching children a very important social skill—sales.

Sales and marketing are often the most sought after and highly compensated positions in the business world and for good reason. They are not easy. In an interview, Cristobal Conde, CEO of SunGard, offered the following words of wisdom: "My advice to young people is always, along the way, have a sales job.... Selling something to somebody who doesn't want to buy it is a lifelong skill."

It is a skill that requires knowledge, good communication, persistence, and confidence—all things needed to be influential. Influence, like sales, is a contact sport. You must be able to communicate effectively, and the more practice your child receives at a young age, the more comfortable sales will become.

Prepare your child to sell, but do not be their scapegoat. Brainstorm where they might find the most willing buyers, how they should initially approach someone, and what to say when they get a yes or no. Reinforce that not everyone is going to buy for various reasons so that they will feel less discouraged by rejection. Role-play the conversation to give them added confidence before heading out into the neighborhood. If your children do not hit their sales goals, life will move on. I promise.

Public Speaking

Public speaking is a consistent, top-ranking fear among Americans, but being comfortable in front of a crowd is an important aspect of influence. Ralph Waldo Emerson once said, "All great speakers were bad speakers first." Being relaxed in front of people is simply a byproduct of practice. Just like sales, the more you do it, the easier it becomes.

While attending a New Year's Eve party in 2013, I noticed the hosts had a large, wooden stage in front of the fireplace in their living room. It was fully equipped with curtains, props, and a microphone. Naturally, it became the topic of conversation as it took up half the room. We discovered their younger daughter loved to sing and dance. They built the stage as a Christmas gift to encourage her to perform elaborate shows for the family. They did not push her, but they found a fun, creative way to inspire her to practice! Not to mention, as the party moved into the wee hours of the morning, the adults may have had some fun on stage as well!

It does not have to be a big, dramatic production however; this can happen at the dinner table. Ask your children to recount their day to the family. Encourage them to discuss the highlights of their morning, afternoon, and evening. Be sure to listen and respond as they talk, letting them know you hear what they are saying. Engaging in this dialog as often as possible is a great start to building comfort in front of a crowd.

CHAPTER FIVE

THE FAMILY MEETING

Up to this point, we have discussed ways to prepare your family for success, but building a long-standing legacy requires an understanding of how to make this process repeatable for future generations. John D. Rockefeller, Jr., wanted to ensure his family's wealth would reach his great, great, great, great grandchildren. He recognized the only way to guarantee future success was by fostering and promoting growth in his family. He accomplished this goal by starting a family office and implementing consistent family meetings to help the next generations manage the Rockefeller fortune. In 2014, nearly one hundred years later, the Rockefellers ranked twenty-fourth on *Forbes'* list of richest families with a net worth of ten billion dollars.

Another noteworthy family continuing its legacy is the UK's Rothschilds. In the mid-eighteenth century, Mayer Amschel Rothschild was one of the wealthiest men in the world. After gaining an apprenticeship under a very influential banker, Rothschild learned everything about the banking industry, foreign trade, and currency. He created his fortune as a rare-coins dealer and then in the banking industry. Rothschild eventually had five sons, who were also brought up learning about finance. When they reached adulthood, Mayer loaned each of them money to build a banking business in one of the era's European financial capitals: Frankfurt, Vienna, London, Paris, and Naples. His sons then would have to repay the loans to the "family bank" so future generations could benefit as well.

As part of the stipulations of the loans, Rothschild charged each child monetary interest as well as intellectual interest. Each son would teach Mayer the information he gained so that wisdom and knowledge could be shared with other family members and friends. Most notably, he created a communication platform for building the family's human and intellectual capital, and almost 250 years later, Rothschild's wealth and legacy continues just like the Rockefellers'.

Follow the Leader

What is evident in many of these powerful families is that raising successful, intelligent, and well-adjusted children has nothing to do with luck. Ensuring your children are set up for success is a matter of having a vision for the future. You, as the leader of your family, must build the platform to communicate effectively and share information as your children grow.

The family meeting has long been the staple of solving problems and making big decisions. Parents call everyone together, the problem or situation is explained, and consensus is reached. But what if there are no issues? Does your family still get together to discuss the future? The essence of a family meeting from a legacy perspective is that it should not need a crisis or big decision to take place. In fact, if done correctly, the family can effectively avoid problems. Thus, the family meeting is the final and most important aspect to building a legacy.

Significance of the Family Meeting

Family meetings are vital to the success of individuals and to the family as a whole. These meetings—held as often as you like—build the structure to effectively help members deal with the difficulties of life but feel the warmth of a great support system.

Families with younger children should start by having brief meetings more often. Anyone that has spent time with young children can attest to their short attention spans. Monthly or quarterly family meetings lasting 10 to 15 minutes would be more beneficial than one or two long meetings annually.

As children become teenagers and then adults, the ability to plan family meetings becomes increasingly difficult. Ultimately, this is where the family meeting falls by the wayside. Yet the need for guidance, strength, and family does not stop at the age of independence. This is where successful families like the Rothschilds and Rockefellers differ from the ordinary; their family meetings continue indefinitely.

As you build the qualities most often associated with successful people (drive, emotional balance, creativity, influence), the family meeting becomes the centerpiece of future growth. If 70% of wealthy families fail by the third generation due to poor communication and planning, the annual family meeting acts as the bridge to reach your grandchildren and beyond more effectively. Frank discussions— especially about finances—continue to be seen as taboo in today's culture. Many parents avoid discussing financial matters with their children because it is uncomfortable. Successful families are bucking this trend, however, openly working together as a team and getting exponential results from a wealth perspective.

While information about the Rothschild and Rockefeller meetings are generally held in secret, and for good reason, the primary focus is to preserve the human, intellectual, and financial capital of the family unit. When family wealth is lost, it is usually the family or the individuals that fail first, not the money. While the objective of these gatherings is to foster family closeness and success, they may also bring to light weaknesses, addictions, or problems. This is great news! If potential problems exist, it is best to discover them early even if it is painful. A family that can effectively deal with negative situations can better ensure against loss of wealth and, most importantly, relationships.

Keys to a Successful Family Meeting

Family meetings are important to creating and maintaining wealth, communication, and intelligence, but how should the meeting be conducted in order to best serve its purpose?

First, it should be held outside of the family home if possible. Making the meeting a weekend retreat or part of the family vacation is a great option. Vacations are an opportunity to strengthen your family culture by doing something unique. If your budget does not allow for a big vacation, taking the family to the local park can work just as well. The key is minimizing the distractions of everyday life. Removing excuses is also vital. "We are too busy" has become the justification we use to combat the fact something has gone unaccomplished. Are people busier today than they were 30 years ago? Sure. However, we make time for things that are important. This phrase is merely a nice way of saying "This is not really a priority." Successful families know the importance of participation and strive to ensure members have good reason to set time aside in their calendars. Choose the best frequency for your family, but for most, annually should be sufficient. If you decide to make the family meeting a retreat, schedule the next two years in advance so the adult members can work around their schedules. Video conferencing technology can also be a last resort if it is impossible to join the group in person.

Lastly, the family meeting is a great time to encourage open and honest communication, but it is not time for a parent-dominated lecture to air your grievances. If the meeting is centered around what you feel is right or wrong with the family, it is unlikely to get a favorable response. Everyone should feel they have a voice and role; otherwise, enthusiasm will eventually fade. Think of your job much like the bumpers children use while bowling. You should provide enough room for the family to determine its path without ending up in the gutter....

Family Values

During the initial meeting, the goal should be to define your family's values. These principles should reflect how the family's identity is to be perceived in the next 20, 50, and 100+ years. Your family's values are the symbol of the group's beliefs, attitudes, and ideals. This is an important step in defining the future, so it is imperative that you take as much time as necessary to get it right.

Here are a few sample questions to get the conversation started:

- What are the primary goals of your family in the next 1, 5, 10 years?
- What are some practices of successful families that you admire?
- What kind of relationship do we want with one another?
- What are my unique talents and abilities that can help the family?
- How do we effectively communicate with one another?
- What are the responsibilities of each member?
- How do you, as a family, want to be remembered?
- What is important to leave behind for future generations?

Keep the dialogue open by reminding everyone their voice is respected, appreciated, and heard. These exercises will be a great opportunity as the leader of the family to better understand what makes each member tick. Once complete, your family values pave the way for the next step—creating your family mission statement.

What's Your Mission?

Every successful company has a mission statement. It is the expression that guides the direction of the company and is the foundation from which decisions are made. Developing your family's mission statement allows members to understand the purpose and intent of the family. It will become the sole expression uniting all members and providing clarity during your annual meetings.

The Rockefeller Family Fund, the philanthropic arm of the family, expresses its mission statement as follows:

> *Rockefeller Family Fund is a U.S.-based, family-led public charity that initiates, cultivates, and funds strategic efforts to promote a sustainable, just, free, and participatory society.*

It later explains in more detail the focus of its efforts:

> *...RFF has worked at the cutting edge of advocacy in such areas as environmental protection, advancing the economic rights of women, and helping citizens hold public and private institutions accountable for their actions. RFF is known for its creative grantmaking, its role as a catalyst in the nonprofit as well as the funding communities, and its record of public policy innovation.*

Writing a mission statement can be a difficult task. Take the time to create something that can be cherished by many generations. An effective family mission statement should be specific, unique, realistic, and memorable. The words should strike a chord with each member. If you find it difficult to get started, I recommend focusing on the values you chose in the earlier exercise. How you choose to express the mission statement is completely up to you, but here are a few anonymous examples:

It can be a simple statement:

Our Family Mission: No Empty Chairs

It can be a paragraph such as:

The mission of our family is to create a nurturing place of order, love, happiness, and relaxation and to provide opportunities for each person to become responsibly independent and effectively interdependent in order to achieve worthwhile purposes.

It can be a creative list:

Care
About the world
About life
About people
About myself

Love
Myself
My family
My world
Knowledge
Learning
LIFE

Fight
For my beliefs
For my passions
To accomplish
To do good
To be true to myself
Against apathy

Rock
The boat, don't let the boat rock me
Be a rock
Be remembered

Family Governance

Once you complete your family values and mission statement, it is now time to focus on the family constitution. Creating structure and rules for which the family operates is important to keeping the peace and operating efficiently. This document sets guidelines for decision-making, conflict resolution and also creates roles for individual members. These rules will act as the lighthouse navigating the family ship back to shore when a storm brews.

The family constitution will be a fairly simple document initially, but as your family tree begins to grow, it will become increasingly robust. It should be reviewed annually with changes agreed upon by members. How are disputes settled? How are financial issues resolved? Do you allow outsiders or in-laws in family meetings? Do they have a vote in decision making? What roles should exist, and how are people elected to these positions?

Initially it will be necessary to create only a few roles to ensure proper governance and smooth operation. The executives—generally the parents—oversee the family meeting, creating the agenda, ensuring open communication and mutual respect, and ultimately making any final decisions. A secretary will be in charge of taking meeting notes and recording decisions made during the meetings. These notes act as a reminder of past discussions and decisions as it will become increasingly difficult to recall details over the course of many years.

Grandparents can play an important role in the family structure as well. They can be great leaders of the philanthropic side of the family as well as maintaining and spreading family stories. Naturally, community service and volunteering become more of a priority for most as they retire. Leading the family in giving back can further build a bond with younger generations and strengthen the transfer of knowledge and history. Knowing where you come from is an important part of building a successful legacy.

Legacy and Heritage Planning

To know where you are going, you must know where you have been. Thus, an important aspect of family success is understanding and recording family history. This helps celebrate accomplishments but also brings to light possible issues that could corrupt the future of the family (addictions, health concerns, etc.). A family autobiography highlights your uniqueness. It also can be a great motivator for living members as they can see their own history being written.

There are a variety of ways to record family history. Interviewing the elders of the family is a great start. Ask grandparents about their parents and grandparents. Utilize the Internet. There are many reputable sites that can help track down ancestors as well as important documents. Some families choose to publish books about their history. Others design websites where each branch of the family tree can post photos, messages, stories, and video of their lives as it happens. Be as creative as you like, but most importantly, make time during each meeting to ensure it is documented for future generations to cherish.

The Pursuit of Happiness

The staple of every agenda and family meeting is the focus on individual development and goals. Each member should have their own book, binder, or file strictly devoted to what they want for the future. Goal development is an important exercise for growing, successful families. Focusing on short-term improvement can have an exponentially large impact on success. It is especially important for children to learn accountability to themselves and the family.

The family meeting's foremost purpose is to help each member in the pursuit of happiness.

Controlling your own destiny is the long-term result of this exercise. By guiding your children in the goal-setting process, you will again gain great insights into their motivations, allowing you to lead more effectively. A great way to explain goal-setting is the well-known acronym: SMART.

- **Specific:** "Study more" is an excellent goal, but "study for one hour each day" is better.
- **Measurable:** This is a function of being specific. The point here is that you know if you accomplished it. Did you pass the history test?

- **Achievable:** A goal should challenge you but not set you up for failure. Make your goals gradual improvements, not grand hopes.
- **Relevant:** Goals need to be important to you. Setting a goal to please someone else will likely end in failure. YOU need to want it!
- **Time-based:** Create an end date. This allows you to stay focused and also create new goals. Keep time-frames shorter than one year if possible.

A SWOT analysis can also create a personal profile to foster further development. Standing for Strengths, Weaknesses, Opportunities, and Threats, this tool has long been used in corporate offices for employee development. The result of this exercise is to celebrate strengths, but also understand that everyone has weaknesses. Being grounded in reality and focusing on improvement are staples of successful people and families.

Understanding each member's strengths and weaknesses is also imperative to encourage teamwork and determine who can help each other reach goals. For example, if Jason needs to improve his grade in math and his big sister excels in this subject, partner them up. As the family adds more and more generations, this can be a big advantage. One member may become skilled in the field of finance, while another may be an excellent doctor. Individuals with diverse expertise can be a great asset for future family growth.

Family Study

Learning about success topics or studying great individuals or families together exhibits the importance of continuing education beyond school. Your family could read and discuss books or articles on emotional intelligence, financial planning, or fitness. You could have each member write a short biography on an inspirational person. Religious study can also be included if this is a priority in your family. A key to the success of this exercise is allowing each member the freedom to choose the topic or person of interest. Then, just like Mayer Rothchild and his sons, have everyone share their findings with the group.

Diversify the way the information is disseminated during the meeting. Perhaps you choose to have everyone write a one-page report or create a presentation to deliver. This is an opportunity to work on influential skills we discussed earlier. It is up to you regarding the length of study, but I would advise that it stays brief and to the point. For example, if you want everyone to study a successful individual, specify the educational outcome by posing a few questions:

1. How did this person become successful?
2. What specifically do you admire about this person?
3. How long did it take to see success?
4. What adversity did this person face?
5. What characteristics can you model to improve yourself?

Financials

When your children are young, you may not feel as though money is an important topic nor would you trust them with confidential information. However, studies show that children ages 8 to 14 are starving for more financial knowledge. For many families, communication regarding money matters is unmentionable. Recently my client, Jane, found out her father was a multi-millionaire when she had to step in as his power of attorney due to his declining health. Jane, now in her 50s, had no idea her father had such wealth and was never taught how to handle money of this magnitude. While this may seem like a terrific situation, there continues to be great stress as she "drinks from a fire hose" learning advanced financial concepts. She has had to help her father develop an estate plan, oversee complex investments, and generally help with everyday expenses. A little communication could have gone a long way and saved Jane from such a surprise.

When your children are young, time should be taken to teach basic financial concepts such as cash management, budgeting, long-term investing, and charitable giving. If you do not feel equipped to do this, take time to learn together, or have a financial professional guide the discussion. You do not need to divulge important financial information at this point, but education is important to future success. When your children finally reach adulthood, however, openness regarding the family finances is imperative.

An uncommon yet important practice of successful families is ensuring all adults have financial plans prepared and shared with the leaders of the family or a trusted advisor. The reasoning behind this is simple. What are the chances you are able to spot potential issues if everything is kept a secret? This transparency allows the executive council to discover troubling symptoms or unearth members that could impact the future wealth of the family. It could be a business that is failing, health issues that may require exorbitant costs, or credit card debt piling up. Avoid disasters and the potential derailment of family wealth by providing honest feedback and support to those members before it is too late.

The basic financial plan should contain information in four key areas: cash management, protection, investments, and taxes. The first focal point should be cash management as it is the basis for all other areas. Here are a few common questions to answer:

1. Is cash flow positive or negative on a monthly basis? Annually?
2. How is debt being managed?
3. Is there enough cash for emergencies?
4. Is the family saving first before spending on discretionary items?

Generally speaking, you should be saving at least 10% of gross income for long-term or retirement purposes. This savings rate over a 20- to 30-year period will create a meaningful future nest egg. A custom retirement plan will provide greater accuracy however.

Another rule of thumb is building a reserve of liquid cash amounting to three to six months of family expenses. If the family has more than one consistent income, you can be closer to the former. However, if the family is reliant on one income, then six months or more is suggested.

Protection planning is the second area of focus. Protection against major medical issues, lawsuits, or catastrophes is important to defending wealth and generally falls into four main categories:

1. Property and casualty
2. Income protection
3. Death
4. Healthcare

Property and casualty, most often known as home and auto insurance, protects against loss of larger assets but can protect you from potential lawsuits as well. In today's litigious society, extra caution should be taken regarding this risk. Professional liability should be addressed, such as malpractice or business liability insurance. As your family adds successful generations, care should be taken to protect all members from these liabilities as they can be a great demander of resources. Address your coverage needs each year, and assess the value of your most important property.

Income protection is another significant, yet often missed category. Pretend I give you a magic money machine that can print dollar bills whenever you need them. Would you leave the machine in the front yard for everyone to see? My guess is you would go to great lengths to protect it—storing it in a vault underground with armed guards, surveillance cameras, and a high-tech security system. Well, the individuals working in your family are the money machines! I find that many people leave their machines exposed to potential loss. Personal and group disability income protection should be a top priority to those generating income for the family. Your ability to earn a living is often your greatest asset!

A premature death could also derail the financial growth of the family as members could be left to fend for themselves or use family resources to survive. Life insurance is key to protecting a family early on as wealth is being accumulated but also in protecting that wealth across generations. Considerations for life insurance include retiring debts, lifestyle continuation, and accomplishing financial goals such as educating children and retirement of a spouse. Aside from the traditional use of life insurance, it can also play a large role in creating a financial legacy, which I will address soon.

Healthcare is the final area of concern in protecting the family fortune. Most have seen just how quickly a medical issue can add up to thousands of dollars in doctor and hospital bills. Chronic conditions can add even greater stress. Every member should have proper health insurance to protect against loss of wealth, but there is another segment of healthcare becoming just as dangerous. Long-term care is quickly becoming an estate killer for many families as our country's largest generation, the Baby Boomers, begin to enter their "golden years."

Costs covered by long-term care policies include adult day care, assisted living, and nursing home and in-home care. In 2013, less than 35% of families with a net worth between $100,000 and $5 million owned a long-term care policy. Many cite that they will rely on their wealth to take care of these expenses. Remember, our goal is to grow our net worth from generation to generation, so those families choosing to self-insure put themselves at odds to see their legacy disappear. Long-term care should be given serious consideration for any member over the age of 40 to protect the growing family fund.

The Family Fund

Warren Buffet, great American investor and businessman, claims to be leaving most of his $72 billion estate to charity. Buffet cites, "I want to give my kids just enough so that they would feel that they could do anything, but not so much that they would feel like doing nothing." Unless you are a billionaire many times over, giving all of your money away is not going to help your family grow its legacy, yet Buffet's concerns are rational. How do you leave money to future generations without corrupting the drive to be better than the last? Enter the family fund.

First, due to the ever-changing landscape of estate law, variance between states, and number of strategies possible, I will not go into detail regarding the actual estate instruments that can be used to create the family fund. Consult with your financial professional, estate attorney, and accountant to find the best way to implement your strategy. The objective here, however, is to paint a broad picture of the purpose of the family fund and how it can preserve wealth.

Imagine your family fund as (hopefully) a large pot of money from which each member can benefit from now and 100 years into the future. Your grandchildren or great grandchildren can use funds to pay for higher education, get a loan to start a business like the Rothschilds, fund philanthropic endeavors like the Rockefellers, or help with unexpected healthcare costs. Notice, however, that none of these examples include buying a new Mercedes or funding a trip to Paris.

The family fund's objective is not to enhance lifestyle but help each member live with dignity and pursue career happiness.

The goal of the family fund, along with this book, is to give future generations the opportunity to successfully pursue the career or life they choose. If your great grandchild wants to be a doctor, get a professional designation, or open a new smoothie franchise, the family fund will be there (assuming they show readiness for the endeavor). Your great grandchild's lifestyle, however, should be up to his success. Remember, the three keys to personal drive are autonomy, mastery, and purpose. The family fund should aid in fulfilling these needs.

Since you are likely the pioneer of your family's success and wealth plan, your assets will be the starting point. Family funds are often started by the selling or gifting of the family business, excess retirement assets, the family home, or life insurance proceeds to name a few. Your starting asset goal for the fund should be at least $1 million although I have seen families prudently start with less. Again, the goal is to grow this asset over time, so the family's use of this money will depend upon the size of the fund.

Growing the Family Fund

How do you increase the family fund while also helping your family flourish? First and foremost, the fund needs to be invested for growth. Naturally, people tend to become more conservative investors as they age, but the family fund is meant to be ageless. Therefore, there are inherent risks in being too conservative with the family fund.

The first risk is inflation. The costs of goods and services continue to rise over the course of time. In 1960, the average cost of a new home was $16,500, a stamp was $0.04 and a gallon of milk was $0.49. In 2014, a new home costs you around $269,000, that stamp will be $0.48, and milk around $3.60. Inflation will slowly erode your family fund's purchasing power if your investment return wanes. On average, you should consider the first 3% of your annual investment earnings to just keep pace with inflation.

The second risk is taxes. Depending on how your family fund is set up, taxation of earnings is highly likely. For example, let's say your family fund is worth $1 million and you earn a 10% rate of return this year, or $100,000. If your average tax rate is 20%, you would pay $20,000 in taxes and keep $80,000 in the fund. Thus, your rate of return after taxes is only 8%. Subtract that pesky 3% for inflation, and your fund technically only grew 5%.

The final risk is a growing family. As I mentioned previously, the use of the family fund may need to be limited depending on the dollar figure and number of family members. As your children have children, you can begin to see how paying for college, making business loans, or giving to charity can erode the remaining 5% of growth we achieved in the earlier example.

When John D. Rockefeller first became a billionaire in 1916, the equivalent value of his net worth today was $30 billion. However, the Rockefeller family is only worth $10 billion today with close to an estimated 200 members vying for their piece of the pie. Over a decade ago, the Rockefeller family started to feel this mounting pain. "Historically our goal has been the preservation of wealth rather than the amassing of wealth, but now that the client base is moving to 100 there is a new emphasis on growth," said David Rockefeller, Jr., one of the many great-grandchildren of John D. Rockefeller. Even the Rockefellers were too conservative in their estimates; thus, a consistent focus on growth investments and how benefits are distributed needs to be at the forefront. Many families start with providing education needs from the fund, giving future generations the opportunity to add other benefits such as business loans or charitable endeavors down the road.

Given these risks, the family fund should be invested to obtain a minimum of an 8% average rate of return. Remember, these funds are not being invested for the next ten years but the next one hundred. A diversified portfolio with higher risk but a higher expected rate of return is more suitable given this time frame. Your rate of withdrawal should then be determined based on the gain of the investment minus inflation and taxes. A 4% withdrawal or less of the total asset value should give you a reasonable expectation of the money lasting long-term but not necessarily growing.

Investing in People

The greatest way to grow the family fund, however, is by investing in the family's human capital. As more opportunities for education and intellectual growth are given to family members, financial success becomes more likely. The return on investment for the family fund is that each member leaves their future estate to the fund just as you will. You invest money to sustain the fund; you invest in people to grow the fund.

How can you make everyone participate? If you have done a good job establishing the purpose of the family, the "pursuit of happiness" mantra, and the annual meeting to ensure proper use of the funds, family members should want to contribute, knowing their future generations will be well served.

If you use the family fund, you should contribute to the family fund.

Contributing to the family fund should be a matter of pride, knowing the use of the money has been well thought out and managed. But what if a member chooses a life path that does not involve great financial rewards? The last thing you want to do is create pressure to make life decisions based on money. There is nothing wrong with members devoting their lives to lower income careers if that is their chosen path.

For instance, your grandson uses family funds to go to a great college, spending $100,000 along the way. In making this investment, you hope he becomes successful and builds a sizable net worth to add to the family fund eventually. But what if this plan fails or he later chooses a career with little chance of great financial gains? Life insurance can be a great way to leverage money and allow each member to eventually replenish what they use.

Implementing permanent life insurance on each individual as soon as they are born can take the pressure off the need to over-achieve financially. The cost is minimal at a young age and can ensure individual contribution regardless of life path. Permanent life insurance generally takes the form of whole, universal, or variable universal life. There are a number of benefits to these policies, including choice of control, growth of cash value, loan capabilities, premium stability, long-term care benefits, and, of course, a tax-free death benefit. The beneficiary of the policy should inevitably be the family fund. Choice of policy and premium strategy will differ depending on your fund strategy, so contact your financial professional for suitable recommendations.

The importance of communicating financial information to the family is paramount. Reiterate family money is not to enhance personal lifestyle but to help each individual pursue their passions and find success. The kind of distributions available are inevitably up to you and the family, but participation in building the fund should be a responsibility and source of pride for every member.

Prepare for the Future

As the Rockefellers demonstrated, a family tree can grow significantly over time, making it difficult to keep up. This highlights why preparation and vision for the future are important. Having a growth plan in place can save a lot of headaches down the road. These obstacles include how to handle larger families within the tree, the roles of outsiders (spouses, professionals, etc.), or divorce.

Imagine how the family tree will change if you have three children and they all have three children and they all have…. Your immediate family tree could easily double or triple in your lifetime!

Because of this, developing leadership committees will become more important long term. Positions and committees beyond the executive council can include:

- Family Bank—to approve the use of family funds and oversee investments
- Philanthropic—to oversee the family's charitable activities
- Personal Growth—to ensure each member is finding success in personal endeavors
- Family Meeting—to schedule and organize the annual family meeting
- Family History—to keep extensive records of all family members and family stories

Continuously updating your family constitution is important for your family to grow safely and securely. Some issues may not be seen in your lifetime, but being able to predict potential problems and establish rules for settling disputes will put your family ahead of the game. The difference between successful and ordinary families is this clear vision for the future.

Have Fun!

While the annual family meeting includes many serious topics, you do not have to settle everything in one sitting. In fact, the family meeting should be just as much about having fun and bonding as it is about taking care of business. Include fun activities such as family game night, picnics, video games, flag football—be creative. Schedule one-on-one activities with each child. Perhaps your son enjoys fishing, or your daughter likes getting manicures. Allow each member to choose an activity *they* prefer, and partner up. Families are meant to be enjoyed, so your final task is to get out and enjoy your family!

CHAPTER SIX

SUCCESS IS A CHOICE

There are many external influences at war against the success of families today. New obstacles are appearing in your children and grandchildren's lives that you never had to face. But you have the ability to equip your future generations with the skills needed to tear down these roadblocks and create a bright and flourishing future.

Building a prosperous family means challenging average expectations. A successful family learns to produce the wealth needed to accomplish goals by focusing on what matters most: personal development and relationships. Successful people are not *born*; they are *made.* They are forged in the tough times, exemplifying drive, emotional balance, creativity, and influence. They often have the support of close family relationships or mentors and understand that success is an unlimited resource. This does not happen instantly nor in a straight, upward path. The road to achievement often gets harder before it gets easier. Is your family prepared for this inevitable dip along the way?

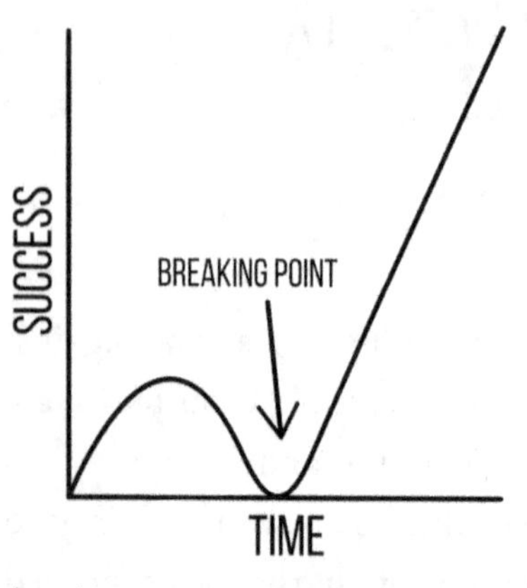

We were all young once. We know the emotional confusion and complexities that go into figuring out who we are and what we want in life. The way you decide to parent can help or hinder your child's development and ultimately, your relationship. Take time to envision the end result for your family and have a plan. Do not let your family fall victim to "whatever happens, happens." It all starts by answering these questions for yourself:

- What is the purpose of your family?
- What are the characteristics you want your children to exemplify?
- How will your family continue to grow 100 years from now?
- How do you want to be remembered?

Work Together, Play Together

Success is not something that one person achieves on their own. It takes the intelligence, hard work, and encouragement of a collection of people. Your young children *need* your support, encouragement without nagging, and limits without hovering. Your adult children need you as a friend and consultant.

The odds are against the over-protective "helicopter" parent. You cannot force success, but you can guide it. Use this book as an outline to awaken the inner drive of your family so they can tap into their potential and create their own version of success. It all starts with your ability to find the right balance. We will always be imperfect, and our family tree will always be "filled with nuts." It is our ability to learn and grow together that dictates where our families go from here. Try to be the example your children need and, most importantly, enjoy the journey!

I wish you all great success!

NOTES

- "Take the Family Dinner Challenge." *The Scramble.* Last modified 2014. Web.
- Luthar, Suniya S.; Latendresse, Shawn J. "Children of the Affluent: Challenges to Well-Being." *National Institute of Health.* February 2005. Web.
- "Drug Facts: High School and Youth Trends." *National Institute on Drug Abuse.* Last modified December 2014. Web.
- Hoyert, Donna L. Ph.D.; Xu, Jiaquan M.D. "Deaths: Preliminary Data for 2011." *National Vital Statistics Reports.* Volume 61, Number 6. October2012. Web.
- Williams, Roy and Pressier, Vic. *Preparing Heirs: Five Steps to a Successful Transition of Family Wealth and Values.* 2003.
- Rev. of *Springboard: Launching Your Personal Search for Success.* G. Richard Shell. Executive Book Summaries. Web.
- Bryant, Adam. *The Corner Office: Indispensable and Unexpected Lessons from CEOs on How to Lead and Succeed.* 2011.
- Bornstein, David. "Hard Times for Recess." *The New York Times.* 4 April 2011. Web.
- Sagolla, Dom. "How Twitter Was Born." 140 Characters. 30 January 2009. Web.
- Sifferlin, Alexandra. "Doctors' Words Influence End-

of-Life Decisions Made by Patients' Families." *Time*. 10 May 2013. Web.

- Mortenson, Kurt W. *Maximum Influence: The Twelve Universal Laws of Power Persuasion*. 12 June 2013.

Chapter 1: Drive

- Pennington, Bill. "Told to Be 'Realistic,' Ted Ligety Defied His Doubters." *The New York Times*. 12 February 2014. Web.

- English, Bella. "Snowplow Parents Overly Involved in College Students' Lives." *The Boston Globe*. 9 November 2013. Web.

- Segrin, Chris; Woszidlo, Alesia; Giveritz, Michelle; Montgomery, Neil. "Parent and Child Traits Associated with Overparenting." *Journal of Social and Clinical Psychology*. Vol. 32, No. 6, 2013, pp. 569-595.

- Business Book Summaries. "Mindset: The New Psychology of Success" by Carol S. Dweck, PhD. 1 June 2010. Web.

- Engle, Marianne Ph.D.; Gurian, Anita Ph.D. "Kids and Sports." *New York University Child Study Center, Child Study Center Letter*. Volume 9, Number 1. September/October 2004.

- Tracy, Brian and Rose, Colin. *Accelerated Learning Techniques: The Express Track to Super Intelligence*. Audio. 21 February 1996.

- French, Michael T., Homer, Jenny F., Robins, Phillip K., et al. "What You Do in High School Matters: High School GPA, Educational Attainment, and Labor Market Earnings as a Young Adult." *Eastern Economic Journal.* 2014.
- Mueller, Claudia M.; Dweck, Carol S. "Praise for Intelligence Can undermine Children's Motivation and Performance." *Journal of Personality and Social Psychology.* 22 December 1997.
- "Involving Children in Household Tasks: Is It Worth the Effort?" University of Minnesota College of Education and Human Development. Revised 8 May 2013. Web.
- "Household Chores for Children: A Guide for Parents." *Family Shrink.* Provenzano, Fred Ph.D. Web.
- "Fidelity Survey Finds 86 Percent of Millionaires are Self-Made." *Fidelity.* 19 July 2012. Web.
- Kuperminc, Gabriel P. Ph.D.; Holditch, Phyllis T.; Allen, Joseph P. "Volunteering and Community Service in Adolescence." *Department of Psychology Georgia State University and the University of Virginia Charlottesburg.* Web.

Chapter 2: Emotional Balance

- Williams, Neil F. "The Physical Education Hall of Shame." *The Journal of Physical Education, American Alliance for Health.* Volume 65 Number 2. P17(4) Page 1.

- Williams, Susan. Rev. of *Emotional Intelligence,* Daniel Goleman. Business Book Review.
- Siegel, Daniel. *The Whole-Brain Child: 12 Revolutionary Strategies to Nurture Your Child's Developing Mind.* 11 September 2012.
- Gottman, John Ph. D. and DeClaire, Joan Gottman. *Raising an Emotionally Intelligent Child.* 1997.

Chapter 3: Creativity

- Meikle, Scott. "Embracing Our Creativity." *Independent School.* Winter 2014.
- Grant, Gaia and Andrew. "The 7 Biggest Creativity Killers." *Fast Company.* 2012.
- Sharp, Caroline. "Developing Young Children's Creativity:WhatCanWeLearnFromResearch."*National Foundation for Educational Research.* Autumn 2004.
- Rev. of *Who Killed Creativity...And Can We Get It Back?,* Andrew and Gaia Grant. Business Book Reviews.
- Gray, Peter. "Children Today Are Suffering a Severe Deficit of Play." Aeon. 14 July 2014. Web.
- Griffith, Susan. "Imaginary Play Life in Childhood Stirs Adult Creativity; CWRU Psychologist Explores in New Book." *ThinkBlog.* 4 November 2013. Web.
- Berlin, Leslie. "Prototype - We'll Fill This Space, but First a Nap." *The New York Times.* 27 September 2008. Web.

- Wagner, Ullrich; Gais, Steffen; Haider, Hilde; Verleger, Rolf; Bom, Jan. "Sleep Insight: Creativity and the Neuroscience of Slumber." *Nature.* Vol 427. 22 January 2004. Web.

Chapter 4: Influence

- Scharlatt, Howard. "How to Influence When You Have No Authority." *Forbes.* 3 January 2011. Web.
- Internet Movie Database. Accessed February 2015. http://www.imdb.com/title/tt0090493/awards. Web.
- Look to the Stars. Accessed February 2015. https://www.looktothestars.org/celebrity/oprah. Web.
- Rev. of *Maximum Influence,* Kurt W. Mortens 152

Chapter 5: The Family Meeting

- Hughes, James E. *Family Wealth - Keeping It In The Family.* 1 June 2004.
- *http://msb.franklincovey.com. Accessed 11 March 2014. Web.*
- *Money Confident Kids.* Price, T. Rowe. Accessed 11 March 2014. Web.
- McDill, Kent. "Ultra High Net Worth Investors Ignoring Long-Term Care Insurance." *Millionaire Corner.* 8 January 2014. Web.
- Hylton, Richard D. "Rockefeller Families Tries to Keep a Vast Fortune from Dissipating." *The New York Times.* 16 February 1992. Web